The **7** Keys of Success

for

Urban Schools

The 7 Keys of Success

for
Urban Schools

By

Dr. Reginald R. Williams, Sr.

ISBN: 978-0-9864397-0-4

Dedication

This book is dedicated to my leaders of learning (teachers) at Kirby High School. It takes a special person to work in an urban school environment. You must possess a unique set of skills. You must genuinely care for students no matter what their background. Every ounce of your energy is dedicated to the progress of your students. I have always told my teachers to take care of themselves first—mentally, physically, and spiritually. I told them if they take care of themselves "foremost," they will be prepared to feed our students mentally, socially, and physically. These teachers work daily on the front lines and because of them, we were able to accomplish something special, as indicated by our moving from the High Priority list to the Reward school list. I dedicate this book to them.

About the Author

Dr. Reginald R. Williams, Sr. has over twenty-five years in education. The last eight of those years have been spent as the principal at Kirby High School in Memphis, Tennessee, an urban school that serves over 1,300 students. Over 80 percent of his students are on free or reduced lunch. The Hispanic population has tripled in the past seven years, and African-American students make up the majority of the student body.

Dr. Williams has earned eight different certifications in the following disciplines: Mathematics 7-12, General Science 7-12, Biology 7-12, Geography 7-12, Earth and Space Science 7-12, Supervisor Of Attendance, Administration and Supervision K thru 12, and Superintendent, but he has spent the majority of his time teaching math and science. He has previously served as an assistant principal at the middle school and high school levels, and as an assistant coach and head coach.

Dr. Williams has received many honors and awards and made over 100 presentations locally, across the state of Tennessee, regionally, and nationally. The award about which he is most proud is a team award: His school was awarded the EPIC Gold award three years in a row for outstanding academic achievement. Dr. Williams told his staff, "We are the only high school this size to be recognized for this type of award not only for one year, not two years, but more."

Even better, before this manuscript went to print, Dr. Williams was notified that Kirby High was recognized as a Reward school. That signifies that Kirby High was recognized as one of the top 5 percent of schools in the state of Tennessee for academic achievement.

Contents

Preface

Initially, I was very embarrassed to write this book. I had to be convinced by several individuals, starting with former board member Betty Mallott and my late friend and motivator Paul Terry, who worked at Remington and Vatterott Colleges before his untimely death, and including national speaker and book publisher Victor Woods. People are brought into our lives for various reasons. Those three individuals came into my life during an eight-year span, and they all stated that my work was worth putting in writing. There is a reason for the season.

Many principals in our area are replaced each year, and I am sure this is a nationwide problem. How can we hire better prepared urban school principals equipped with the necessary tools, as well as unique skills, to survive the long haul? I hope I can offer a little encouragement or advice for anyone presently serving or seeking employment as an urban principal.

Acknowledgements

I would like to thank former Board Commissioner Betty Mallott, who said privately to me in 2007 after my first year in the principalship that I should consider writing a book about my successes at Kirby High School, located in Memphis, Tennessee. Honestly, that was the furthest thing from my mind. I would like to acknowledge my fraternity brother in Atlanta, Georgia, public school administrator Billy Ware, for telling me recently, "Ever since I have known you during our college days, you never cared what people thought about you —you stayed focused and driven and you continued to treat people with respect even though they were throwing darts in your back." I also would like to acknowledge national speaker and book publisher Victor Woods for encouraging me that this next step could be done.

I earned my doctorate as I was serving as the principal of one of the top ten most populated urban schools in Memphis, Tennessee, and I had to take graduate classes throughout the week and sometimes on the weekends to keep my sanity. My dissertation chairperson, Dr. Stephen Marvin, had confidence in me, supported me, and encouraged me when things got tough at work, in graduate school, and with the regional or district offices. I also want to recognize both of my editors, Linda Beam and Mildred Murchinson. Their ability to make sense of my grammar while keeping the book real is a unique gift both of them possesses.

Introduction

Most urban school environments deal with a myriad of challenges and issues such as neighborhood conflicts, harassment, bullying, intimidation, sexual orientation, fighting, homeless students, students moving four or five times within a school year, and foster parents enrolling three or four different kids into school within the same calendar year. Common discipline issues include dress code violation, tardiness, class cutting, marijuana (being under the influence or having intent to sell), bringing backpack(s) of items to sell on campus, and insubordination, just to name a few. There are academic issues such as students being overage for grade, students with IEPs, high failure and ultimately high retention rates, and high teenage pregnancy. Most recently, social media issues have plagued the educational environment in a negative way with concern over cell phones, which bring problems of their own. These include pornography on cell phones, cheating with cell phones, and students calling people to the school on their cell phones to settle problems, not to mention social media messes involving Facebook, Twitter, and Instagram (to put it mildly) that permeate our building and result in conflicts and fights. This social media epidemic is threatening to ruin a generation of our students.

No one outside of the educational community cares about those conflicts and challenges; most feel that if high school principals are making six-figure salaries, they just want results, no excuses, which some in the educational circles frame to our teachers as, "No excuses, but results." Educating our students is a high-stakes business. Accountability for this task is at an all-time high. Principals are losing their jobs. We must increase graduation rates and increase test scores. Our job as urban school principals is very complex. A plethora of negative issues with teachers, parents, alumni, and community activists can keep you off track of doing the most important task, educating students. I have always said urban principals are only two or three bad news stories away from losing our jobs if the poor test scores don't get us first.

To meet the responsibilities of this weighty position, principals need all the help they can get from as many resources as possible. This book offers practical, proven advice based on on-the-job experience that will help any urban school principal prepare for the tasks that lie ahead.

PRINCIPAL

Visible

Accessible

It's usually not the technical skills where principals have difficulty; it's the human relations skills. Personal relationships.

Train Assistants

Chapter 1: The Principal's Role

This book will examine seven ideas or areas in which urban school principals need to be successful in order to move their school academically, culturally, and socially. But first, let's take a look at the role of the principal. The first two letters in the word *principal* are PR. It is appropriate that when we think of the letters PR, we may recall that they often stand for "public relations." This is directly applicable to the role of principals. The process of relating to the public is a vital one in a principal's job.

When I first arrived at my newly appointed school, I immediately visited area stores, businesses, and churches within a 1-mile radius. Later, I reached out to those areas that were within a 2-mile radius. I attended PTSA meetings, site-based meetings, monthly meetings at the Hickory Hill Police Precinct, and sporting events. You must sell your program. You must sell your school. You must become the face of your brand. For good or bad, you must lead.

Foremost, you are a servant. The work of a principal is fast paced, complex, fragmented, and sometimes isolated. Given this kind of environment, it is very difficult to make sense of a principal's work. He or she must be a trained observer; confidant; keeper of secrets; sifter and sorter of knowledge; pacesetter and routinizer; referee; linker of people, ideas, and resources; financial broker; translator of school policy; paper pusher; accountant; clerk; disciplinarian; and moral authority. You must be visible and accessible, including to students.

Personal Relationships

One of the most important facets of a principal successfully leading a school is within personal relationships. And yet it is human relation skills, not technical skills, with which most principals have difficulty. Principals ultimately received their appointment from the superintendent but they must earn the respect from their staff in order to be successful. There is a cliché' that states if the principal sneezes, the whole building catches a cold. In other words, what affects the principal may also affect the school. That's why it is important that in his or her role as the instructional leader, the principal's attitude is consistent, without constant mood swings. The principal will occasionally experience an impromptu interaction with an unpleasant parent before they go into a meeting. They may encounter students' disturbances in the hallway, but before getting on the intercom, they must keep their emotions in check. They must avoid as much as possible, emotional highs and lows that affect people around them. Hence, when the principal sneezes, the whole building catches a cold.

Principals must train the leaders around them and develop their talent to maintain stability. There is a big difference in making recommendations (as an assistant coach, assistant principal, copilot, or vice-president) compared to sliding one seat over and making the ultimate decisions (as head coach, principal, pilot, or president). Again, there is a big difference in making the recommendations to making the ultimate decisions. Educators and staff must be properly trained for those broader roles.

Accountability

Principals serve as the CEO of their schools. The dynamics today in which they work can't be duplicated. They don't know what to expect each day. One major dynamic about the composition of their job as CEO is that they are held accountable for things that occur in their buildings when they aren't even there. By analogy, principals who make a list of the things they hope to accomplish on any given day could be derailed by a bad incident anywhere in the neighborhood.

Here are a few distractions that urban school principals may encounter on a weekly if not daily basis: someone calling the main office and saying a bomb is in the school, an irate parent or an unruly student, an investigation involving inappropriate contact between a teacher and student, a relationship gone bad between teachers, a tip involving a possible weapon in the school, an incident resulting from a teacher failing to properly supervise their classroom, a student recording something inappropriate on their cell phone within the school, and/or an SRO (school resource officer) coming to the administrative staff about an immediate concern that could jeopardize student/staff safety, just to name a few.

Trust me, there are many, many other incidents that could easily derail you from your list and keep you from your main responsibility, which is getting into the classrooms and giving teachers the support they need in order to get the proper gains from your students for your school to be successful. Accountability is no joke.

It takes a special and unique individual to work within an urban school setting. As an educator, I definitely don't have anything against teachers who work in a different environment. It takes all of us to help meet different and unique challenges to prepare all of our students for the future. But in an urban setting, a principal takes on the roles of psychologist, father, mother, coach, social worker, counselor, preacher and teacher.

Managing Stress

It is critical that principals serving at urban schools take care of themselves emotionally, physically, and spiritually. As the late North Carolina State Coach Jim Valvano once stated, "To me there are three things everyone should do every day. Number one is laugh. Numbers two is think—spend some time in thought. Number three, you should have your emotions move you to tears. If you laugh, think and cry, that's a heck of a day." I would advise all administrators not to take the stress of the daily job home with you.

I realize that's easier said than done. I learned it for myself in a dramatic way. It was the winter of 2008; I was dealing with two or three difficult staff members, I was in the middle of my doctoral degree taking Statistics II and III, and I was dealing with challenges from my own biological children with issues in their lives. I vividly remember waking up and going through my daily routine. As I was brushing my teeth, began to spit and it was coming out sideways. I repeated the process and I felt peculiar. I immediately looked in the mirror and my face, especially my mouth, was slightly twisted. The left side of my face was slumped and my left eye was watery. I immediately thought I had had a stroke. As men sometimes do, I made a stupid decision and went to work anyway, and some of my staff members noticed my facial muscles were different. I went to the doctor and they gave me some medication and said I had "Bell's palsy," which had symptoms similar to a stroke. The stress of the job can be unbearable, especially if you are working under adverse conditions such as having an unappreciative boss, trying to work with an untrusting or ineffective administrative team, managing more than your fair share of poor teachers, dealing with self-servicing alumni or community activists, and receiving unexpected visits daily from unappreciative and irrational parents. But principals must find ways to manage the stress before it manages them.

Interacting With Parents and Students

As an urban school principal, I have dealt with parents who wanted to post pictures of their child in the hallway because the child was a runaway. We deal with sixteen- and seventeen-year-olds in the ninth grade. We deal with the eighteen-year-olds in the eleventh grade that are not making the grade. We deal with the nineteen-year-olds in their senior year in high school. We deal with the seventeen-year-old female that has two babies and her parents have put her out of the house, so she is living with the boyfriend's parents or her mother's parents. Have you ever seen a parent and a child arguing during a conference in front of an administrator? All of these complications make it difficult for a student to obtain a high school diploma. Furthermore, these ambiguities make it more difficult for the principal's school in reaching their graduation rate as mandated by the state department. The principal must use all their resources (i.e., graduation coaches, counselors, school psychologists, family engagement specialists), and involve the students' parent(s) to ensure that child graduates. However, if you are a smaller high school and your district's or school's budget is minimum at best, you will not have these resources available. Even in the absence of ideal resources, the principal must still find a way to help the students graduate.

Leading an urban school can cause you to wake up at three or three thirty in the morning and not be able to go back to sleep. My alarm clock is set to go off at five o'clock each morning. It has only gone off twice in eight months. Somewhere I heard that people who wake up with a purpose don't need an alarm clock. Since I am totally focused on the daily grit and grind of my schedule as a principal, I cannot lose focus that I am directly and indirectly responsible for the education of 1,500 students. In an urban school setting, principals are losing kids that they have never seen. The dropout rate is tough to stomach at times, and to complicate matters, principals are dealing with teachers who may know their subject area or content area but need additional professional development and sensitivity training in dealing with the challenges of urban children. An example would be a conference I attended entitled "What to Say and How to Say It." This conference addressed another critical area of a principal's job, knowing what to say and not say during student, parent, and staff conferences. It is important that administrators be trained in what to say during these meetings and what we should or should not say during all conferences. Sensitivity training is needed for teachers and staff that will provide the do's and don'ts of what to say during student or parent conference.

Not only can saying the right thing facilitate the goals of such meetings, but correct communication can prevent problems from arising from incorrect communication. Principals are often held accountable when a teacher or staff member misspeaks. I have often had to put out fires that someone on my staff ignited. To set the correct tone, and make sure that everyone is on the same page, it has been my policy to meet with my entire staff, including cafeteria and custodial staff, to let them know my expectations of how they should deal with students. It is especially important to communicate this with not only staff who will deal with students directly, but even those whose contact will be minimal or indirect, such as in after-school hours. Providing proper training to professional and support staff can preempt problems in this area.

Chapter 2: The Four Rs: Relationships, Responsibilities, Respect, and Results

Most principals' dismissals can come in many facets. The average tenure of a principal at a large urban high school is three to five years. One of the most important integral elements in being a principal is maintaining the four Rs. The four Rs stand for relationships, responsibility, respect, and results. We are cordial in our relationships with our stakeholders. We are taking care of our responsibilities (i.e., following policy). We are respecting everyone even though our constituents might not like the answer, and finally, the results. Are our students making the grade? Are they passing the state exams? Are they competitive with other schools? Our parents, teachers, and students can deal with our shortcomings and our faults, but if principals get the four Rs right, life still will be difficult but your tenure will last longer.

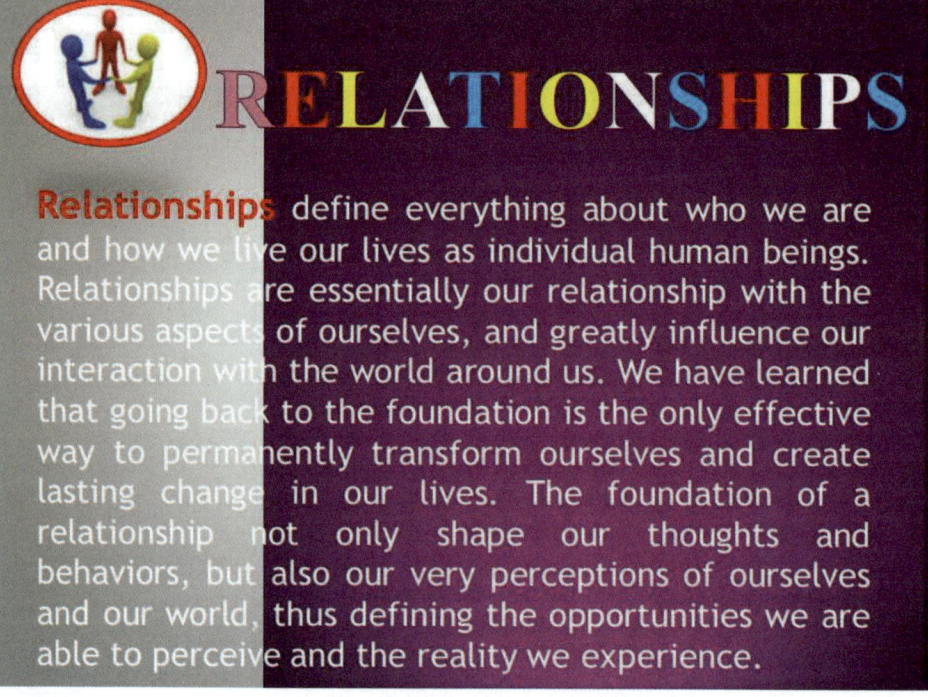

RELATIONSHIPS

Relationships define everything about who we are and how we live our lives as individual human beings. Relationships are essentially our relationship with the various aspects of ourselves, and greatly influence our interaction with the world around us. We have learned that going back to the foundation is the only effective way to permanently transform ourselves and create lasting change in our lives. The foundation of a relationship not only shape our thoughts and behaviors, but also our very perceptions of ourselves and our world, thus defining the opportunities we are able to perceive and the reality we experience.

Relationships

Successful teachers understand, students don't care how much you know unless they know that you care. Once you reach them, you can teach them. For the most part, as the lead administrator I honestly trust people, but I don't trust their private thoughts. If adults aren't about the children and they have their own personal agenda, their mask will eventually come off and students will see their true agenda or purpose.

An urban school principal must be committed to dealing with difficult situations. No circumstance is harder than dealing with the untimely loss of students or faculty members. I have had to deal with the death of two teachers, three current students, and an untold number of former students. My grandmother once told me a parent shouldn't have to bury their child. I have witnessed this at several urban schools and it hit home when it was a basketball player I coached or used to coach or a student I was presently teaching. As principals, we all have a human side that deals with relationships in schools and the tragic losses that go along with the job.

I have received phone calls during school hours concerning a student who has lost a parent or a staff member who had lost a loved one. The principal is the critical catalyst in helping everyone survive the loss, especially when that loss is a current faculty and/or staff member or a current student. I have spoken at numerous funerals of students and former students.

I must admit one of my key attributes is dealing with parents. Over 95 percent of my parents just show up without an appointment. I make sure I genuinely address each parent's concern(s). Sometimes, amazingly, after I listen to a parent talk, I realize they really didn't want anything. They just wanted someone to listen to their concerns. Assistant principals, please don't get unraveled or offended by this, but some parents will visit their child's school and only want to speak with the principal. I was taught that lesson as an assistant principal: We are here to support the principal of the school.

As the leader of the school, my pressures don't come from the superintendent. My pressures don't come from the area or regional superintendents, nor do my pressures come from teachers or parents. My pressure is self-induced. Foremost, I want to find solutions to every problem. I want that parent to leave my office realizing I have done the best I could for their child. I want that teacher to feel that I heard their concerns. I have tried my best to solve every problem within my building so the parent wouldn't need to contact the regional or superintendent's offices. Of course that was a challenge at times, but again, every decision that we make has to be student centered. Not adult centered, but student centered. What is in the best interest for that child? By your asking that question, the parent knows you have the interest of their child in mind and they can't use profanity or become unruly towards that concept.

One Saturday night around eleven o'clock, I received a call from security that the police department had been dispatched to my school concerning a possible break-in due to the alarm being activated. When I arrived on the scene, the officers told me that an individual had been found sleeping in a portable, and he had identified himself as a former student. He was in the police car when I arrived. When I went to the car, the former student spoke to me and apologized for the inconvenience. I immediately recognized him though I had forgotten his name. He said he was homeless and that his parent had left town and he couldn't get into the house. I asked him why he was sleeping in this portable. He identified that portable was used as an ISS room when he was in school three years ago and by forcing the door to open, he didn't think it would set the alarm off. I immediately believed him. I told him as he sat handcuffed in the back seat of the police car to come and see me once he was released. He did. He asked me if I would accompany him to court for unlawful entry and see if the court would dismiss the $750 fine since vandalism did not occur. Weeks later, he came to my school and I took him to court in my car. This is called building relationships.

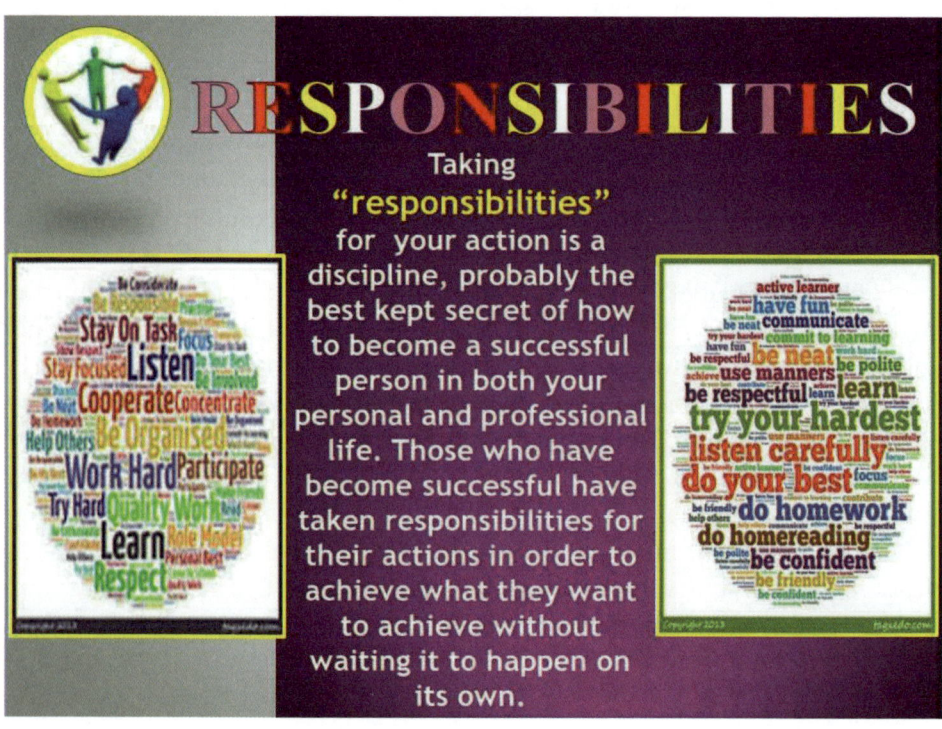

Responsibilities

We have a responsibility to educate every child. We have the responsibility to provide a safe environment. We have the responsibility to report a "Trust Pays" tip to the proper authorities. We have the responsibility to have courageous conversations with individuals (teachers and staff) within our building if they are not measuring up.

We have every responsibility to check out a tip that a student brings to us no matter how trivial it may seem and how much it pulls us from our other responsibilities. Societal ills have brought X-ray machines and metal detectors into every high school. Random locker and classroom searches are the norms. We have the responsibility to report neglect and abuse of our children without the parents' consent. Some of our students are practically raising themselves due to parental neglect of basic responsibilities toward their children.

Some students do as they please at home, and those are the students who have trouble abiding by school rules. Because they run their houses, they think they can come and run the school. Those students are usually in for a rude awakening and in some cases, they don't survive in a traditional high school setting.

We have a responsibility to run our schools by following and enforcing the doctrine of MBWA, which stands for Management by Walking Around. Administrators will learn a lot more by walking around than by sitting behind their desk. Principals of urban schools must be visible and proactive. My students and teachers have constantly told me that I am all over the place. I was very visible as an assistant principal. I learned early on that if you walk into any school building and students are constantly in the hallways, it was an assistant principal's problem.

From an administrative standpoint, we are in an age of accountability. In the '60s to '80s, administrators were focused on the three Bs: books, buses, and butts (when paddling was acceptable). When we went to high school in the '70s and '80s, we would assume or guess who the bad teachers were, but today in 2014, we have data to support those claims. As the principal of my building, if I were to ask my teachers, "How many of you are good teachers?" I am sure many, if not all, teachers would raise their hands. But if I were to ask, "How many of you are effective teachers?" now we would have data to support those claims. The accountability factor has caused many urban principals to lose their jobs. We must make decisions based on data, not emotions. As principals, we are criticized for wanting to hire or keep teachers who are a good fit. We want teachers who are competitive and versatile. We want teachers who are team oriented and team players. In the professional sports, coaches and general managers realize if you aren't a good fit they trade you. Their job is at stake. As principals, we are the CEOs and we want teachers in our buildings who will bring good results. If not, we are gone.

As a principal, I have had the responsibility of putting together my administrative team. During my twenty-five years in education and working in six schools, I have seen six administrative teams work together. Some were effective and some were not as effective. In assembling my "dream team," as I affectionately called it, I wanted individuals around me who were stronger in areas where I might have been weak. I was criticized for saying this early on but I knew if I was going to have some sustainability in this environment, I had to use this philosophy. I was blessed to learn at an early age whatever you do in life, surround yourself with smart people who will argue with you. Of course, you have to be confident enough to permit such arguments. You don't need a lot of passive individuals around you or "yes people." Weak leaders surround themselves with yes men who are afraid to argue with them. Real leaders must understand that recognizing your weaknesses and turning them into strengths is a major part of the plan. Leaders must be secure in who they are.

For administrators, primarily principals, it's lonely at the top. Teachers have their colleagues in the building, the secretarial staff members have their colleagues in the building—you know where I'm going with this: Custodial, cafeteria, and administrative staff have their colleagues, especially in a large urban school setting, but the principal is all alone. I must admit that principals have a sense of paranoia at times, and too much of it is not healthy. As I stated earlier, you must trust people close to you, but what I don't trust are their private thoughts. If that administrator isn't loyal to you or has a hidden agenda, you will eventually find out through their actions.

Another accountability piece has a student's twist. One spring several students were preparing to take the AP exam. One counselor came to my office and said one male student was a no-show. This student was an honor student and the counselor and teacher felt something was wrong since he wasn't present. I told them to make a phone call. I was informed he was up all night due to problems at home, and also, he had no way to school. I went and picked him up and he immediately started explaining what had occurred at home. I calmly told him, "Get your mind ready for this exam and you will be alright." I asked him, "Have you eaten?" and he replied, "No sir." I took care of his appetite, and he went and took his AP exam. I would like to call this section Taking Ownership and Being Responsible!!

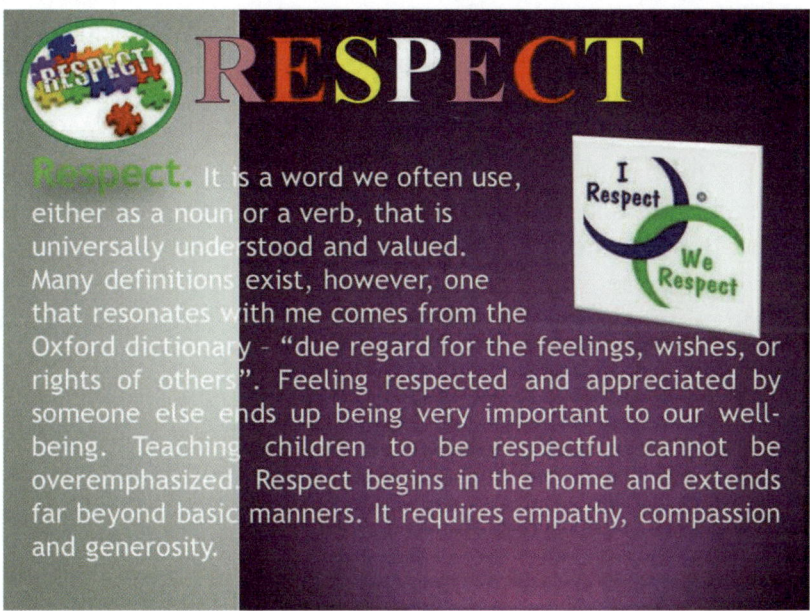

Respect

As urban school leaders, we hold positions of power and influence that can help our community's children realize and experience true democracy. Whether we are trying to strengthen instructional skills among teachers, gain effective strategies to support a safe school environment, build relationships with families, or identify ways to use data to support decisions and expand resources, we must create a school that will assist everyone and effectively support the school environment. It is easier to build strong children than to fix broken men.

When I was a former high school coach, kids would literally run through the wall for me. If I asked kids to jump, they wouldn't ask why. They would ask how high. Other coaches would always observe and tell me that my basketball players played hard for me. As a coach, I knew that if kids know that you care for them they would do anything for you. That same philosophy applies to your teachers and staff: If they know you care, they will do anything for you. They will do the little extra things around the school for you. They don't want the school to fail because of your leadership. Teachers and staff realize as the principal you get the credit for success but you also get the blame for failure. I remember a book that I read entitled *If You Don't Feed the Teachers They Eat the Students!* by Neila A. Connors. I made sure I kept my teachers' appetites satisfied. I would sometimes allow my teachers to dress down on Fridays. I would provide lunch for them in the teachers' lounge, or place a small token of appreciation in their mailbox. I might also mention their name(s) on the intercom or at faculty meetings for positive things that they had done. I would send them to a professional development session that they requested so they could improve their craft. If one of my teachers was having a bad emotional day, I would excuse them to go home. I would rather send them home than to have that teacher escalate matters and become a legal issue. Trust me, from an administrative standpoint, that teacher and your staff will never forget appreciative and supportive gestures. I would never intentionally embarrass a teacher in front of their colleagues and especially the students. There is an old church phase: "You can't raise a man up by calling him down." I am trying to develop future leaders and certainly mistakes will be made. Calling a teacher or staff member into my office to make professional corrections privately goes a long way.

Furthermore, I remembered that some of my teachers were also parents and needed time to nurture that important role too. If their own child was sick, or if their child was involved in a school play, I would always try to take care of my staff if it was reasonable. I always remembered the saying, "People don't care how much you know, they just want to know that you care." I cared for my staff.

When I first entered the principalship, I formed a teacher advisory board. It was a board that brought questions and concerns from other anonymous faculty members, and they would take turns reading those questions to me. I had a recorder to write down my response to each question. I didn't want this board to be a rubber stamp or become a griping session. At the conclusion of the advisory board meeting, I would have someone type and print responses and place them in everyone's mailbox. This was my way of being transparent and letting the other faculty members know the tough daily decisions that I had to make and my reasoning for making them. They ultimately realized that all of my decisions were student centered. I would like to call this section, You Must Show Respect in Order to Get Respect.

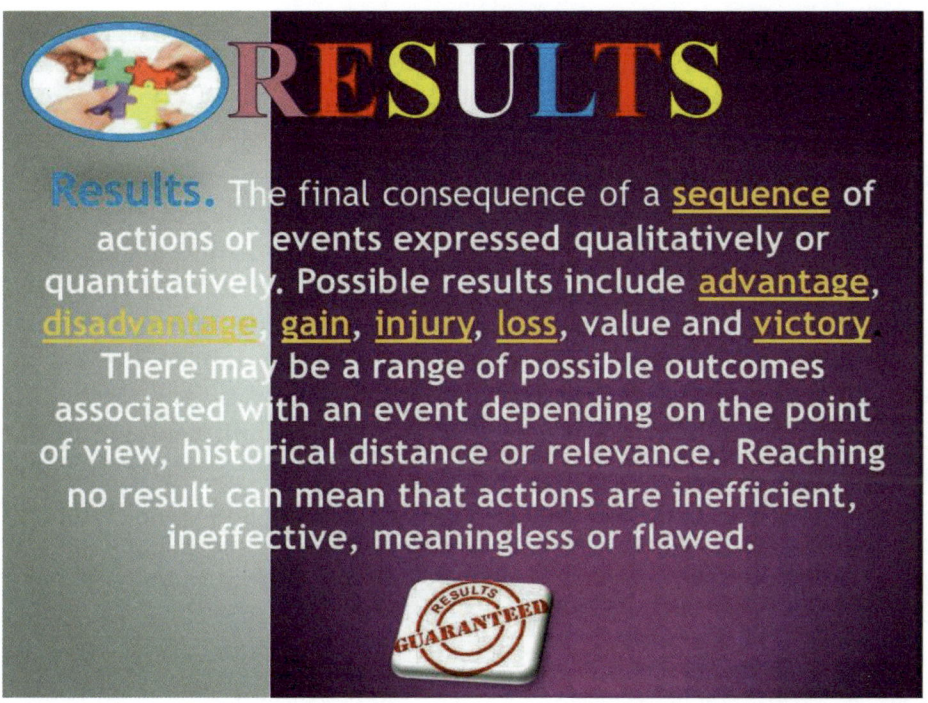

Results

Just as any organization sets goals and expectations, the same thing should be done for sports teams, schools in general, and various committees within that school. There should be a plan to accomplish those goals. As French writer Antoine de Saint-Exupery said, "A goal without a plan is a wish." We don't want our students wishing for anything: "I wish I could be a teacher," "I wish I could be a lawyer," or "I wish I could be a doctor." We tell our students to put those ambitions on paper and orchestrate a plan in achieving that goal. That would be your end result. When I was coaching I used the five Ps: Proper Planning Prevents Poor Performance. This same concept can be used for teaching. Our teachers shouldn't shoot from the hip. Most successful teachers plan their lessons. They have a plan for struggling students or students who need interventions. They have an enrichment plan for students who catch on fast or get through early with their assignments. Educators realize accountability is at an all-time high. We must find several ways to assess our students. Successful teachers assess their students several times throughout the lesson. We told our teachers to inspect what you expect. In other words, in preparing for a weekly test, don't wait until Thursday to inspect what you expect your students to know on Friday's text. The same applies waiting until March and April when you know your students will take the state-mandated exams in May.

We must teach our students that they will fail more than succeed in life. To prepare for it, they must plan their response to it. My personal failures were the initial driver's test I attempted at the age of eighteen. My younger sister and I went at the same time and she passed the test on her first attempt. What a blow to any older sibling's ego! I often speak with seniors who had a rough time with the ACT test. Most of them would make a score in the range of 15-17, but the 18 or 21 score would be elusive for them early on. I often tell a personal story of how I made a 13 on my ACT. Some students are amazed at this and wipe tears from their eyes. Based on my own experience, I felt I had the responsibility to set up ACT remedial programs so the students would not have to encounter the same thing. We initiated ACT tutorial sessions after school and on Saturdays so they could improve their initial scores. We also hired an outside agency that instituted a day-long ACT prep session for selected students.

Another failure I encountered was with the NTE (National Teacher Examination); today we call it the Praxis test. I received rejection letters from undergraduate schools and later on graduate school admission programs. Other temporary setbacks I experienced were interviews that I went to and subsequently received a letter stating, "Thanks for your interest in our company, but you were not selected as a candidate; best of luck in your future endeavors." Life is not about how we handle success. It is about how we handle failures. We must constantly tell our students this. You must get up more than you fall. You have heard the slogans, "Failure isn't an option" and "You will fail more than you succeed." To illustrate that failures are common, but can be overcome, I have shared the following facts with students on several occasions to illustrate how this has been true in the lives of two famous people.

> He lost his job in 1832.
> He was defeated for state legislature in 1832.
> He failed in business in 1833.
> He was elected to state legislature in 1834.
> His sweetheart died in 1835.
> He had a nervous breakdown in 1836.
> He was defeated for Speaker in 1838.
> He was defeated for a nomination for Congress in 1843.
> He was elected to Congress in 1846.
> He lost renomination in 1848.

He was rejected as a land officer in 1849.
He was defeated in his run for the U.S. Senate in 1854.
He was defeated in the nomination for Vice President in 1856.
He was again defeated for the U.S. Senate in 1858.
He was elected President in 1860.

So you have suffered a setback? You are not the only one to have failed. The statements above occurred in the life of **Abraham Lincoln**. Like Lincoln, our next individual didn't stop after a setback.

He missed more than 9,000 shots in his career.
He has lost almost 300 games.

On twenty-six occasions, he was entrusted to take the game-winning shot and missed a lot more than he hit. This statement describe the sports icon **Michael Jordan**.

The moral behind the stories of these two extraordinary individuals is <u>not to stay down</u>! And it is not just famous people that have a story to tell. The homeless person has a story to tell. The substance abuser has a story to tell. The guy you see asking for "spare change" at the intersection has a story to tell. Maybe, just maybe, they fell so many times they never got back up. And yet even their failures to keep on keeping on serve as an important illustration of what can happen when you fail to keep trying. The lesson here is that the result of any effort will be entirely dependent on your approach and willingness to <u>never give up</u>!

Our students need to understand that they will fail more than they succeed. Educators everywhere should help pick our students up when they fail. We need to tell our students that if they fall down four times, get up five times. If they fall down eight times, get up nine times—don't stay down!

I must admit when I first arrived as the third principal in four years, making AYP or AMO wasn't a great concern in my first full year. I felt if I had an environment that was conducive to learning, the small things would be corrected easier. In this section I will include ten quick hitters that I executed with a result in mind.

First, I put up large banners stating **"Under New Management."** I wanted to change the culture and mind-set within the school. I also wanted to inform parents, stakeholders, and community leaders alike that change was here (Result 1).

I felt when new principals are appointed they make one major mistake: They come in making too many changes and fighting too many battles. For my sanity, I knew I should address unruly students first and students overage for grade and put parameters in placed for consequences for their negative behaviors (Result 2).

I addressed parents' and teachers' immediate concerns. I had my teachers identify and write two things on an index card that they liked about their school. Secondly, I asked them to give me two things they would like to change at their school. I personally responded to each teacher's concerns in writing (Result 3).

I had my first parent meeting. Over 400 parents showed up. The "Under New Management" signs resonated over the entire building. I explained to parents my open door policy and my expectations. I identified my "Tipping Points" (Result 4), which I'll say more about in Chapter 7.

I also wanted to communicate those expectations to our student body. I had multiple assemblies by gender for ninth graders, tenth graders, eleventh graders, and twelfth graders. That was a total of eight assemblies. I wanted those assemblies to be up close and personal. I repeated my expectations on the intercom and various communications throughout the school. Students knew what the consequences would be if they violated the Tipping Points (Result 5).

Early on I addressed every parent whose child returned from a three-day suspension or more. I also asked the administrator who suspended the child to be present for this meeting. I wanted the assistant principal to be present and see how I communicated with that parent. This was especially important during my first month at this school. Fighting would immediately result in a minimum of a ten-day suspension, depending on the circumstances. I expelled many students who had a history of fighting, especially those who continued to fight after I arrived (Result 6).

I initially asked the teachers for a list of every student that was two academic years behind or two years behind based on age or grade. I arranged a bus tour to GED and Job Corps programs. The tour included two coaches and at least fifty students. I set up Parentlink for parents, placed communications on our Web site, and sent information home by students saying that failure was not an option. I informed students that if they were two grades behind, statistically they had an 80 percent chance of dropping out of school altogether. This was a reminder of what was stated in Result 2, but at the same time, it stated the consequences of dealing with a student that was unruly and overage for grade (Result 7).

The administration staff and coaches controlled the hallway at the tardy bell. Hall sweeps went into effect. Students caught in the hallway sweeps without a hall pass were given an immediate consequence, which was an overnight suspension. This suspension was denoted as a conference with the parent to get them involved immediately before something big occurred (Result 8).

I had a meeting with all staff members who had morning duty roster/responsibilities such as the metal detector/X-ray machine entrance (cafeteria) and hallway supervision as the students left the cafeteria and headed to their first period classes. That list also included school personnel assisting with tardy students. I eliminated attending homerooms daily. I had a list devised for lunch duty roster/responsibilities. This included the cafeteria and hot spots throughout the building during lunchtime. Finally, I also had dismissal duty roster/responsibilities in the afternoon, which included inside the building and outside the immediate campus (Result 9).

Each assistant principal was put in charge of two programs of work (POWs).

- Administrator A—English 9 and Algebra I
- Administrator B—English 10 and Algebra II
- Administrator C—English III and Biology

I tried to assign each assistant principal with a program of work they were certified in or what's reflected on their undergraduate and/or graduate hours on their transcripts. Our administrative meetings occurred once a week and we focused on instructional items first, even though operational items eased to the forefront at times. These instructional teams met whenever necessary. Every Wednesday, we had some type of PLC (Professional Learning Communities) meetings. The second and third Wednesdays were dedicated to academic departments and instructional leadership team meetings. The fourth Wednesday was dedicated to professional development, and the first Wednesday of the month was our general faculty meeting. I also produced a weekly Calendar of the Week. This document included all activities that would occur for that week. I didn't deviate from this weekly agenda. Instruction was first (Result 10).

I personally carved out these ten actions where the groundwork was laid. This foundation ensured positive results and we celebrated small successes.

Chapter 3: Legendary Leadership—Legendary Service

Legendary Leadership

Legendary Service

The classified staff can make or break your school. They have thankless responsibilities. It is very hard to clean up behind somebody. The building engineer, custodial staff, secretarial staff, cafeteria staff, school resource officers, guidance counselors, hall monitors, paraprofessionals, family engagement specialists, and other support staff, depending on the size of your school, have very important responsibilities as they relate to running an effective urban school. I don't take their job responsibilities lightly.

Sensitive Situations

These individuals must be caring and sensitive to students' needs, and they must be blessed with skills to de-escalate situations. My secretaries must be able to work in stressful situations. In high school environments, our attendance and main offices are the two areas that have a high volume of traffic. It is important that the staff there monitor who is checking out certain students. They deal with visitors, stakeholders, and parents alike. They must handle a high volume of sensitive materials. Some parents may come into the office wearing pajamas, hair rollers, and a bathrobe or gown with house shoes. Some parents may come into the office wearing something that's too revealing. We are all public servants. I don't need anyone from our school saying anything derogatory or offending anyone due to how they look or dress. There have been times when I have informed a parent one-on-one that what they were wearing was too provocative and should not be worn in an educational environment. It all depends on "what you say and how you say it."

Our school had a history of arresting parents or banning them from campus before this administrative staff arrived. I can say only one parent has been arrested under my leadership. I spoke with the parent before her arrival and I asked her to report to the main office and ask for me. Needless to say, she went into another part of the school and things escalated. Furthermore, I have only had to ban one parent from our campus, but we ended up resolving the matter several weeks later for the betterment of her child. I can honestly say, in eight years I had only one parent to use profanity towards me personally, and that was in a phone conversation that I ended abruptly. Most parents, if not all, ultimately want the best for their child. The major challenge for us as administrators is finding the common ground without losing face and/or compromising our principles.

80/20 Rule

Principals need their staff members to address parents that might be upset when they come into your school. You want secretaries that will de-escalate situations, not add gasoline to the fire. Establishing positive relationships with your parents and stakeholders alike is important. Every school should take 100 percent responsibility in advocating for legendary leadership and legendary service. All successful organizations — businesses, civic organizations, churches, and especially schools —have an 80/20 rule. Usually, when eighty percent of the organizations is moving in the same positive direction, you will get positive results. But we need everyone carrying the load, not just 80 percent. Some will even debate that it's much lower than 80 percent that does the work. Whatever the ratio, everything should still be student centered.

As the graph (Figure #8) shows, you have individuals who make up four distinct "bones" within that organization. You have the jawbone individual. They are always talking about what should be done but they do nothing. You have the wishbone individual. They are wishing someone else would do the work. Next, you have the knucklebone individual. They are always knocking someone else's ideas and criticizing everyone's idea but offer no suggestions or solutions. Lastly, you have the backbone of the organization. They are the individuals carrying everyone else and doing all the work. Every organization, large family, or church group has these individuals.

Successful Organizations... Successful Schools
Ex. 80-20 Rule

4 Distinct Bones

Jaw Bone   Wish Bone

Knuckle Bone   Back Bone

Canoeing

Rowing

Riders

Drillers

Figure 8

Another way of saying this is that in any organization, everyone should be rowing in the same directions. You have individuals that freeload – they are simply there for the ride. We call these people riders. Sadly, you also have the drillers. These are the people who try to sabotage your programs. They are constantly putting holes in your projects. They are trying to persuade other people to follow them. They don't want you to succeed. As a school leader, the challenge is getting the riders to be independent thinkers and getting the drillers to be part of the program or out of your building.

Accessibility

I make every effort to set an example of service in my dealings with parents and students. For example, although I do not encourage impromptu parent conferences, and I do not advocate them for other administrators, 95 percent of my parents just stop by the main office to see me. They don't schedule an appointment. If the wait becomes too long, my secretary will inform them that if they would like to schedule an appointment the principal will do his best to honor the appointment time. I make an effort to return all phone calls and/or e-mails within twenty-four hours. In order to put out fires in advance and to remain proactive, I have given my personal cell number to my PTSA president and alumni president.

I try my best to be accessible to my students. Some students see me in the hallway and ask me, "When is the best time to speak with me?" But a few students drop by the office unexpectedly to see me. My policy for the students is that they may come by during their lunch period or after school, or they may stop by with a hall pass during class. From the first few minutes of the conversation with the student, I find out if I need to get a counselor or additional support staff to assist me with the student.

In other words, legendary leadership and legendary service have to start and come from me. Everyone on my staff knows that I have an open door policy. If a student felt they were being mistreated, they would honestly tell a teacher, "I am going to see Dr. Williams." When the student came to me I would always address what that student should be doing first. I don't take sides. I would even call the child's parent before the child got home so the story would be told the correct way. I would not change a student's schedule based on perceptions and innuendoes. Before I considered changing a student's schedule, I always had a conference with the teacher, parent, and student. I always tell my teachers to make sure you make contact with the parent first. It was always tough for me to defend a teacher with a problem student in their classroom if the teacher hadn't made documented contact with the parent first. We all must be on the same page. Teamwork makes the Dreamworks.

Another reminder of Teamwork makes the Dreamworks occurred a few years ago, when our region was experiencing triple-digit temperatures when school had begun in August. Since most of our students walked to and from school daily, I felt as the instructional leader I needed to do something for our student body as they prepared to walk home. I consulted with the financial secretary and building engineer and purchased small bottles of water and placed them in barrels of ice prior to school dismissal. You should have seen the looks on the students' faces when the dismissal bell sounded and when they exited the school to see ice-cold bottled water waiting on them as they left. Everything schools do should be student centered.

Excellence in Service

The toughest part about this section is that legendary service must be given to everyone on your staff, even the ones who are out to get you. If the leader isn't fair or doesn't possess a kind heart, his or her supporters will see it and they may swing to the other side. Legendary leadership must deal with difficult staff, toxic staff, and toxic gossip from your staff. The latter issue may be especially challenging and it may take special effort to "tame the tongue." A few years ago during an in-service, I gave each teacher a copy of some wise words and explained to them why it was important to identify and avoid all negative staff members and to avoid toxic conversations that could derail us from accomplishing our goals.

Taming the Tongue
(James 3:3-8, NIV)

When we put bits into the mouths of horses to make them obey us, we can turn the whole animal. Or take ships as an example. Although they are so large and are driven by strong winds, they are steered by a very small rudder wherever the pilot wants to go. Likewise the tongue is a smart part of the body, but it makes great boasts. Consider what a great forest is set on fire by a small spark. The tongue also is a fire, a world of evil among the parts of the body. It corrupts the whole person, sets the whole course of his life on fire, and is itself set on fire.

All kinds of animals, birds, reptiles, and creatures of the sea are being tamed and have been tamed by man, but no man can tame the tongue. It is a restless evil, full of deadly poison.

The leader must also deal with individuals who love to make life miserable for the rest of us. With the proper training, workshops, professional development, and a strong mentorship program, eventually, you will learn why they act the way they do. You will find out exactly what to say and do in specific situations. You will see how to bring out the best in even the worst offenders.

Finally, legendary leadership will show how to coach that staff member up to your expectations or coach them out of your building. Again, we all must be on the same page. Teamwork makes the Dreamworks.

Everything should be student centered. Every school should aspire for Level 5 leadership. Level 5 leadership defines exemplary service. The ratings or rubric indicates the individual is performing significantly above expectations. An old cliché' that's used in educational circles is that you can either coach them up or coach them out. If an administrator or teacher is performing below level (Levels 1 or 2) and the ineffective educators who are performing below expectations want to improve their craft through professional development, mentoring programs, and staff development, ultimately we can coach them up. But if the opposite is occurring, we must coach them out because our students are the ultimately ones suffering. Of course, I don't have anything against teachers, teacher unions, administrators, parents, or other external factors, but if you have a school that's more passionate in other internal or external factors and those goals and initiatives take you away from the main objective—-students—-your school won't be successful. As the bull's-eye in Figure 9 shows, everything should be student centered. Your students, your scholars, should be the center or the major focus of all your decisions.

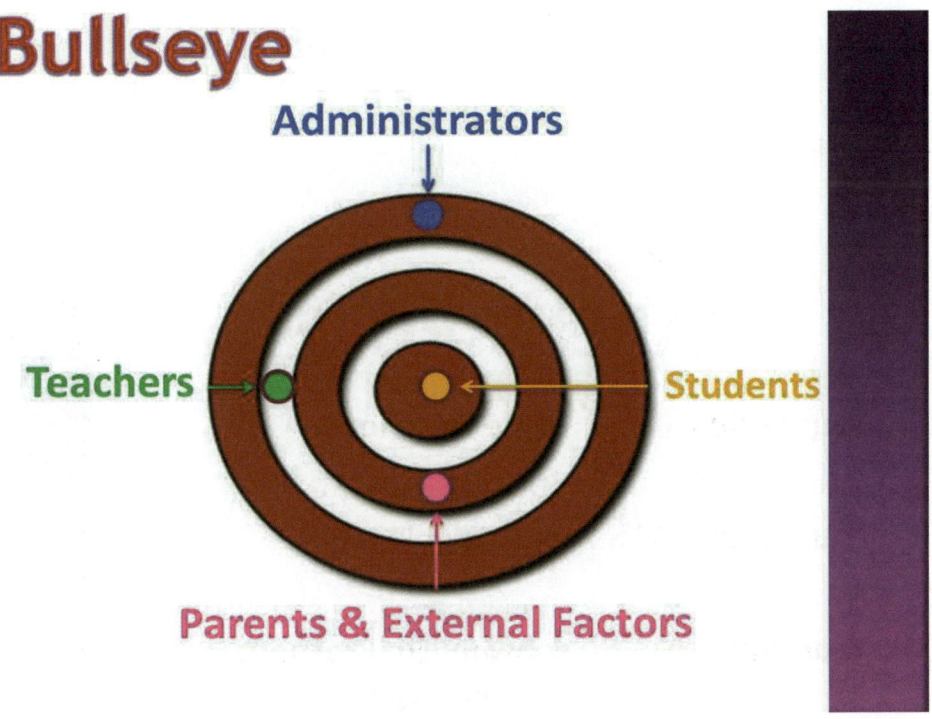

Figure 9

Chapter 4: Parents' Role

PARENT ROLE

- Your child **MUST** come to school

- Your child **MUST** go to all classes

- Your child **MUST** show mutual respect
  "yes sir" ... "no sir"

- Your child **MUST** put forth his/her best effort

As the lead administrator, I ask my parents to make sure their child does four simple things:

Your child MUST come to school.
Your child MUST go to all classes.
Your child MUST show mutual respect
        (using "yes sir, no sir," etc.).
Your child MUST put forth his/her best effort.

I always told my parents to make sure their child makes it from the bus stop to the school stop. I emphasized to parents that because their child leaves home, that doesn't mean they will necessarily make it to school. We need parents more concerned about coming to the school to get a progress report or report card that didn't make it home instead of coming to school acting irrational over a confiscated cell phone.

Offering Resources

Even though parents' frustrations seem to be directed toward the school, most of the time that's not their true source of frustration. Most parents are frustrated instead with their child, and as urban school principals, we need to come up with the resources to support that frustrated parent. These resources could involve the counselors, whether with school sessions or outside counselor agencies; use of our family engagement specialist, who also has outside agencies to reach out to; or we could refer overage children to an academy, prep school, Job Corps, or GED program, depending on their age, number of credits, and overall career interest.

I had a student who walked into my office and said it was his mother's fault that he was getting suspended. He was getting suspended for excessive tardiness to school and said his mother was not waking him up on time. I asked him purposely, "How old are you?" He said, "Seventeen." I told the student, "I have an eighth grader at home and I don't wake him up." He was frustrated and wanted to drop out. I asked him, "Where is your mom?" Since he was angry and late, I gave him my personal alarm clock from my desk. I told him to take it home and bring it back tomorrow with his mom so we could discuss his future. I left Mom a message on her phone. The student returned the next day with his mom. Oh, yes, he had the alarm clock that I gave him under his arm as they walked into my office. However, a few weeks after the conference, the student didn't stay in school. He became a statistic.

I recall one weird case in which a student came to school smelling like marijuana. As the student waited for his suspension paperwork, their parent arrived and was adamant that the student didn't smoke it. The parent said she had been smoking it herself while the student was riding in the car on the way to school. Go figure! The student was still suspended; maybe next time, the student will find a different ride.

Getting Students Back on Track

As an administrator, you must put yourself in the place of the parent and trust me, they can feel if you are genuinely concerned about the welfare of their child. You cannot look down on that parent or question why they made poor choices in raising their child. That parent is already aware of their shortcomings and the dynamics of their broken family structure that have failed to provide them with the emotional support they need for their child. I would simply ask, "Mom, dad, grandparent, even the foster parent, how can I help get your child back on track or how can I assist you and help get your child back on track?" A parent can't curse at that.

The purpose of a parent conference is to bridge the gap between the parent, child, and school. When parents come to the school, most of them have their own preconceived ideas about what is wrong with public education or most importantly, what is wrong with the school their child is currently attending. A typical conference that I head consists of me sitting in a conference room next to the parent and child. I normally don't like sitting behind my desk because it serves as a barrier to some parents. I want to present an appearance indicating to the parent that I am their ally, not their adversary. As a parent myself, I realize parents' frustration when they invest in something and they don't get the results or outcomes they expected. That leads to disappointment. If the disappointment is not addressed, it leads to frustration. Individuals only become frustrated in something if they have invested time in it. So that irrational parent isn't upset at the school; that parent is upset or frustrated with their child in which they have invested time. Since I know this, I welcome parent conferences and to some degree I enjoy them.

I usually start off by addressing the child's age (if overage for grade), their discipline history, and their overall academic performance. I sometimes ask the child, "Do you love your mom or dad?" In some cases they get emotional. I ask them, "When is the last time you told your mom that you loved her other than her birthday or holiday?" I sometimes use the analogy of a house on fire and ask the student to imagine how the police and EMR in many cases hold the parents back from running into the house to rescue their child or children. I then ask the child to guess, in most cases, which parent is usually the one being held back. I reiterate that although I am a father too, and I love my children, in most cases they are holding the mother back, restraining her from running into the burning house to get her children. I tell the child there is a bond between a mother and child that I would never understand. Moms love their kids unconditionally. Now, why do you take your mother through this process? Inconveniencing her? Clearing suspension? Making poor grades? Having poor attendance? At this point, both of them are emotional and now the direction of the conference has changed from the school's fault to their child's own poor choices.

After exchanging constant dialogue for a few minutes and hearing the student's perspective, I ask the student, "What can I do as a principal to get you back on track?" I urge students not to rush to be an adult and inform them that their adulthood will be much longer than their childhood, so they should enjoy their childhood as long as possible. I reiterate and ask Mom or whomever, "What can I do for you to support you and your child?"

You can't talk down to a parent. Now the parent's frustrations and anger that were directed at the school or an administrator have been redirected. I want to make sure at the conclusion of that conference that we are all on the same page and set up some parameters so that we could follow up with the child appropriately, including referring to other professionals such as school counselors, psychologists, or teachers.

Parent Conferences

Every parent wants the best for their child. I don't care whether that parent has a third-grade education or a PhD. It's paramount that the educational staff-the secretary, counselor, family specialist, psychologist, school nurse, and administrator-treat that parent with respect. Again, every decision that's made should be student centered.

I had one parent come into my office to clear a suspension when her child had used profanity toward a school employee in the cafeteria. The mother's question to me was, "You gave my daughter a five-day suspension for cursing out a cafeteria lady?" My response to her was,

"Yes, that cafeteria lady is an adult, she is someone's mother, and she should be respected by every child in this building, including your daughter."

I had a situation in an urban junior high school in which a parent walked briskly into the main office wearing a long trench coat when she stated she needed to see her son immediately. One of the school staff members asked her to take a seat; her response was no, she would stand. As I was completing some paperwork, I could see a male student walk into the main office. While I watched with my peripheral vision, Mom rushed in her son's direction and started hitting him immediately in his head area and shouting, "Where is my money?" While several of us ran in their direction, Mom's trench coat came open and she was wearing nothing beneath the coat. She came to school completely naked except for the coat and shoes she had on. Mom was arrested for simple assault, and we had to call the paramedics to check on her son.

During several parent conferences, I have sometimes asked a student in front of his parents, "How many ears did the Lord give us?" The student would answer "two." I would follow up with, "How many mouths did the Lord bless us with?" The student would say "one." My point is that the Lord wants us to listen more than he wants us to talk. I always use my own kids to drive home a point. I often recall my successes and challenges as a father and what my mother did for my sister and me as our sole financial provider. I would also point out to the student that the Cs on their report card represent "average." You can't make it in this world just being average. You must be better than average if you want the finer things out of life. I continue by telling that child that life for your mom is stressful enough with working, paying bills, and providing for you and your siblings. But bringing her to this school for unnecessary stuff is undue stress. God forbid, but I would ask, "What would you do without your mother if the Lord took her tonight?"

In an urban school environment, especially at the beginning of the year, administrators try to collect as much lost revenue as possible. I remember an occasion when a parent owed over $200 for her child's lost textbooks. They came into my office while Mom was carrying a baby. I asked her to have a seat and we discussed what books were not turned in by her child. Mom became visibly upset and looked over at her and said, "You know you are going to pay this back to me," and then she began using profanity. Mom gave the baby child to her daughter and without a blink of the eye, and to my amazement, she reached into her bra area (between her breasts) and pulled out a large cell phone and placed it on my desk. She started to retrieve other items from between her breasts (i.e., tissue, a baby's pacifier, ink pen), including money that was balled up and wrinkled. I could see the money was moist. I was stunned. Her daughter looked at her, and Mom was still using profanity while placing items on my desk. Without hesitation, I told Mom she could collect her items she had placed on my desk and she could keep her moist money; I would record this as none collected.

On another occasion, I was having a parent conference with a rude child. According to his mom, he came into the house at night when he got ready. He was failing all his courses. He never brought books home. He was a very bad influence on his younger siblings. He talked back and disrespected his mother, sometimes using bad language. I asked Mom, "Have you ever called the police on him or gone to juvenile court and filed 'unruly charges' against him?" I asked her if she had a life insurance policy on him. I told her if something happened to him, it would only cost about $6,000-$9,000 to put him in the ground. With his eyes big and to his amazement, he said, "What are you trying to say?" I continued, "Mom, I know we hate to bury our children, but he is on his way." I paraphrased a Bible scripture from Ephesians Chapter 6: "If you disobey your parents your life on this earth will be short." Mom wiped a few tears and left with her son. Every now and then, I would see him in the hallway with books in his hand and ask him, "How is your mom doing?" You should have seen the look on his face. The moral of this story is this: Parents should assist their child in picking out the college they would like to attend, not picking out the color of the coffin to put their child inside.

Parent Friendly Programs

Let's face it, when most high school parents visit their child's school, it's for a negative occasion. For the most part, when parents visit their child's elementary or middle schools, there are more assemblies, plays, fund-raisers, parent and grandparent luncheons, dances, honor assemblies, and so forth. By the time the child makes it to high school, a lot of parental visits are to the student services office, main office, or attendance office to clear suspensions or attend a conference with an administrator. In our urban school, we initiated two programs that were parent friendly.

Since our school name began with the letter K, we introduced Kurbside Konnection. This was a project that teachers volunteered for in the morning (when parents were dropping their child off for school) or afternoon (when parents were picking their child up after school). Volunteers walked up to the car and gave each parent a goody bag (consisting of bottled water, drink, or orange juice, with peanuts or assorted mints, candy, and other supplies) and an agenda (newsletter) of what was occurring for the next month. We had a few student leaders holding up signs, and as the lead administrator I was always there. The event usually lasted two days and was a great way to meet parents in a positive setting.

The other project was called Curriculum EOC Family Night and Report Card Pickup. Believe it or not, some high school students' report cards don't make it home to the parent. This event had many variables. First, the parent had to get the report card from a certain location. Second, the parent and student had to visit all classrooms that had state-mandated exams at the end of the year. I asked each teacher to have a dialogue with each parent and discuss with them three key questions:

1. What does proficient look like in this class?
2. Where is my child now as it relates to being proficient?
3. What do I need to do as a parent (in order to assist you in getting my child proficient)?

Each teacher in that subject area had to place a sticker next to the subject on the child's report card. Once the parent/child had visited all classes that required a sticker, they would bring that report card to the parent center to get a wristband so their child could dress down on a designated day prescribed by the principal. Sometimes, we would have refreshments for parents (cafeteria) and hot dinner for the teachers (teachers' lounge). PTSA information would be passed out. The parent center coordinator would pass out information about ACT/SAT, after-school tutorial sessions, and minority students' information (i.e., Hispanic or ESL information). We would have an interpreter on site. If the teacher wasn't in attendance, the parent could fill out an information sheet for a teacher to contact them or to set up a parent conference. Even though I couldn't make this report card pickup mandatory (three times per year), over 90 percent of our teachers would set time aside to see families when in most cases we would not see them at all. Parents would be waiting in line at school's dismissal for the report card pickup to start. Everyone benefitted: the parent, the teacher, and lastly, the student. My philosophy behind this was you can't lead the people if you don't love the people. You can't save the people if you don't serve the people.

Chapter 5:
How Little Things Make a Big Difference

There is never a dull moment in an urban school setting. As the administrator, you must be prepared for the unprepared (unexpected) and realize that no detail is too small to warrant your attention. It is the small things that add up to make a big difference. One afternoon my building engineer called me on the walkie-talkie and his voice had an upsetting tone. I responded to him and he told me to rush to the boys' restroom on the far end of the building. When I arrived inside the restroom there were large red letters written on the wall that stated, "The Crips run this schol not Mr. William midyet ass." The idiot misspelled two words and my last name. I looked over at my building engineer and I said, "If you laugh at that inscription you are fired." Of course I was joking. We immediately closed the restroom down until the walls were cleared. Like I stated earlier, there is never a dull day in an urban school setting. During a three-year period, we have had entire community power outages that affected our building before school started, during school hours, and after dismissal while tutoring and after-school activities were taking place. You must have a plan for the unexpected.

Carry-In Problems

I always applauded my teachers and administration team for remaining focused on academic issues in an area where society's ills crept into our school daily. Our teachers and staff did a marvelous job of catching "carry-in" problems. Those are problems from things that occurred in the neighborhood overnight or over the weekend. Fights, drugs sales, dysfunctional families, and neighborhood conflicts can permeate your school if your staff hasn't been adequately trained to catch these types of problems. One of my teachers had a sign outside her classroom door that read "Drop Your Drama at the Door." Maybe that sign should be placed outside each entry into the school building. We have had at least five fights within our school walls involving family members (mother-daughter and/or father-son) during instructional time. During these tense moments, my teachers remained professional and continued educating our students. There was an incident that occurred in my presence when a daughter struck her mother first and they both became entangled and were eventually restrained from each other. The daughter was placed in handcuffs, but once the officers called the incident into their precinct, Mom was immediately placed under arrest because she had a previous warrant. Mother and daughter were both arrested.

Each school is responsible for ensuring that students experiencing academic difficulties are identified as early in the school year as possible, and appropriate intervention strategies are used to assist students in performing on grade level. When the school is a failing school, and is not meeting students' needs, the problem of poor student performance is compounded.

A lot of our schools in urban communities take on society's ills. For instance, a store was reportedly robbed not too far from the school, and a passerby notified police that the perpetrator was headed toward our school with a gun in his waistband. We were notified as 1,500 students were passing classes. Our school went into immediate lockdown. Can you picture the circumstances that we had to go through? Making sure all hallways were clear. Making sure all teachers checked their roll. We personally went by each teacher's room that had a substitute teacher in the room with an office-generated roll and identified our students in each classroom. The lockdown took nearly an hour to make sure the perpetrator didn't enter our school.

On another occasion, we received an anonymous call that a bomb was in our school. We had to go into lockdown mode for forty-five minutes to check all packages that had come into our school within the last twenty-four hours. We had to check all closets with suspicious or unopened packages. That's additional instruction time we lost.

In another disturbing situation, a student mixed some type of chemical during lunchtime that set off a cloud of dust. The residue burned a few students' eyes in the immediate area. We had to evacuate the school and call EMS and the fire department. Later, the communications department at the school board was notified and shortly thereafter, television cameras showed up. That's additional instructional time we lost.

In another lockdown situation, a student reportedly had a gun on campus, but after the investigation, the weapon was found to be located behind the football /track field area. The weapon never made it onto campus, but we must take every tip seriously. We were under lockdown for over an hour. This incident made the news. Again, that's more instructional time we lost.

An urban school principal's main fear is making the news negatively due to tragic circumstances. Therefore, it is imperative that we try to address situations before they blow out of control. Hence, you lose more instructional time trying to investigate, substantiate, and notify all parties involved because ignoring any detail could bring legal ramifications. Additionally, all of these incidences not only cost time individually, but the cumulative effect of time lost was significant. Even seemingly small losses of time add up to bigger losses that can impact the school's mission. But no matter what happens, we keep focused and remind our students, "We are in it to win it!"

Perceptions of Teachers

Another example of how little things make a big difference would be the Tripod survey, which is used as the framework for effective teaching. Affectionately, it's known as the seven Cs, which are listed below.

1. **Care:** Show concern and commitment.
2. **Confer:** Invite ideas and promote discussion.
3. **Captivate:** Inspire curiosity and interest.
4. **Clarify:** Cultivate understanding and overcome confusion.
5. **Consolidate:** Integrate ideas and check for understanding.
6. **Challenge:** Press for rigor and persistence.
7. **Control:** Sustain order, respect, and focus.

This survey measures the stakeholders' perception of how the students feel about their teacher. Generally, students are happier, harder working, and more satisfied with their achievements in classrooms that rate higher on Tripod's measures of the seven Cs.

Even though this is a survey based on perception, it is only a small percentage of the teachers' evaluation tool. I must admit that teachers who scored low in most areas did have relationship problems within their classroom. The instrument measured perceptions of the teacher having too many referrals or classroom issues, being mean-spirited toward the students, or not caring about the students' well-being.

Show Me Your Friends and I'll Show You Your Future

Student mobility in an urban school is a complex issue. It is another area that can take a cumulative toll on student achievement. And no wonder. Some families move three to four times a year. They move so frequently that when we ask for their student's cumulative records from a previous school, they have left our school by the time the records arrive. Even one move may be disruptive to a student's learning, but when there are multiple moves, the impact is compounded.

Our administration team and teachers tell our students it is one thing to have an F as a grade on your report card but it's another thing to have an F on your record. One F stands for failed, which can consequently be made up, but the other F stands for felony. That F leaves a stain on your character and consequently it is very hard to remove, hence making it tough to find employment.

Every child that drops out of school is a statistic waiting to happen. Statisticians can predict how many jails or prisons to build based on poor reading scores of third and fourth graders. Building jails and privatizing their operations has become a billion dollar industry. Once these students fall behind one grade in elementary school and another grade in middle school, then by the time they reach the ninth grade, they are two grades behind. A student that's two grades behind has an 80 percent chance of dropping out of high school.

Most potential dropouts hang with or spend time with people who are not interested in school. There is a phrase that states, "Show me your friends and I will show you your future." In other words, be careful of your associates. As a former coach at three urban schools, I had players, students, and/or former students who were incarcerated and their own parents would not go and see them but the parent said to me, "Coach, you can go, but I am not going down there." By their own admission, the parent was either too tired or it was too painful to go.

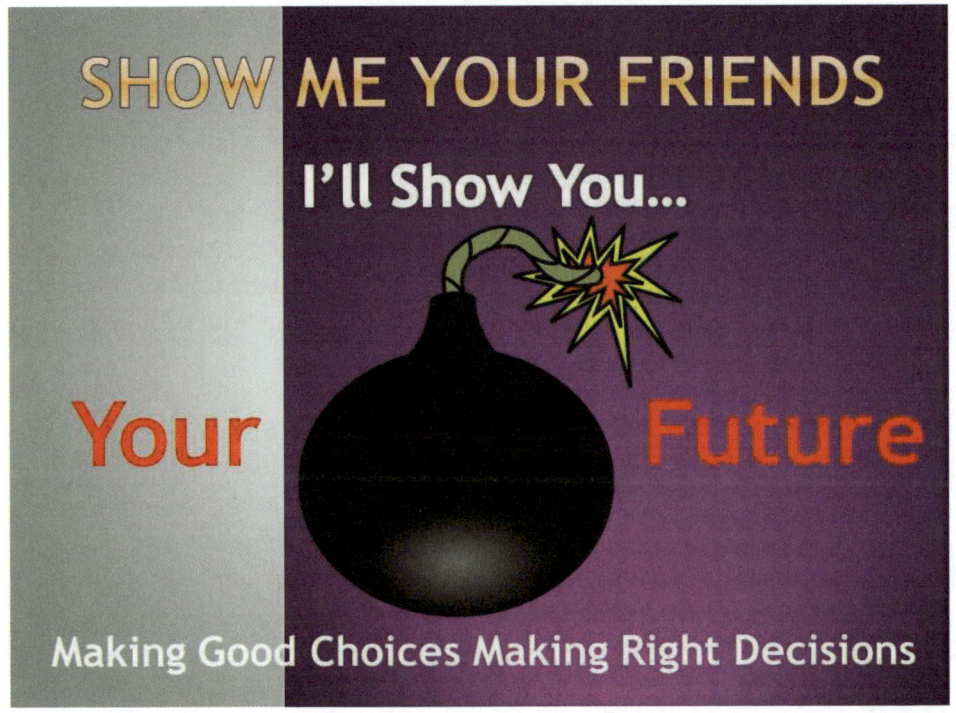

Effective Teams

As I stated earlier, my motivation is solely self-induced. I don't like losing. I am a competitor. I hire good people. I want people around me I can trust. I want people around me that have strengths that I don't possess. An urban school principal doesn't need to have an ego because if you have the same qualities I have, I don't need you. To have an effective team, I need people around me who are strong in areas where I am weak because you are only as strong as your weakest link.

During my years on interview teams before I became an administrator, and especially as an administrator, I made it a point to hire strong men in inner city schools. These men served as a catalyst to help ensure our boys got what they might not be receiving at home. I strategically placed these men's classrooms among hot spots within the school buildings. I assigned them morning duties, lunch duties, and dismissal duties in high-profile volatile areas within our building and sometimes outside on the campus. I attended meetings of the local neighborhood police departments and got their assistance outside our school campus during dismissal. Our coaches and at times the administration staff would personally walk over to the stores next to the school during dismissal and see with whom our kids were loitering at the stores and possibly looking for trouble. I also communicated with the neighborhood businesses for their support.

During my tenure at Kirby High, I have received several letters from students on many occasions, but one in particular hit home. Some of our students write like they text so you must understand when I received a letter that was typed and the grammar and punctuation were superb, I was quite surprised. This letter was received during my first year as a principal.

Dear Mr. Williams, I am a fellow student who attends Kirby High School. I am writing this letter in regards of other students as well as myself to inform you that some of the teachers here at this school are not really educating us in the appropriate manner. My classmates and I feel that we should be taught by a teacher with passion and dedication for his/her students, but we don't feel that way about some of the teachers that work here. Basically, we are asking you simply to talk to the teachers about their behavior towards students and their actual involvement in helping us succeed to the next level in our life.—Anonyms [sic]

I would tell my teachers, if you have an ideal school that hits the mark (academically, socially, culturally) you would allow your own kids to go there. Some of the teachers who had their own child at our school would make sure that they were in the "correct" classrooms, or should I say, in an effective teacher's classroom. As time moved on and as our staff got better, this practice was less prevalent.

I must admit schools are under a lot more scrutiny today than they were ten, twenty, and thirty years ago. Parents should not need to stand in line all night to get their kids into effective schools. All schools should be good or effective schools. If parents show the same passion at these so-called failing schools rallies by attending their local PTSO meetings, parent conferences, open houses, getting involved in their child's education, and supporting the principals' and schools' mission, the chances of a school failing or school doors being closed because of perennial poor test scores would be unlikely. Every parent wants the best for their child. I would tell my staff, repeatedly, if the parent has a third-grade education, he or she still wants the best for their child.

Classroom Procedures

Some classroom procedures may seem insignificant but they are a vital part of an effective school environment. I would tell my teachers to check roll each class period and twice if they had a class during split lunch. This may seem like a small procedure, but it can become a legal issue if it is not done with validity. Several years ago, we once had four male students to leave campus and break into a house. Since this occurred during school hours only three of them were apprehended and charged with a felony. They gave robbery detectives fictitious names. Needless to say, their school's attendance was checked. Three teachers had accurate attendance and one teacher didn't, and it's safe to say that teacher is no longer with the district. I went on record to say to our teachers in a not so humorous way, "I don't care if you teach every day, but 'dammit' you better make sure you check roll every day and each class period."

As a coach I used to tell my players in the locker room after a victorious game, respect the victories. Always remember how it feels in the other locker room. This way you will respect the hard work you have put into this sport. I also used that same philosophy with our teachers and administrative team. If you are good, don't tell everyone, they will tell you. I also used to tell people, "Be wiser than others but don't say so." If you are good, trust me, people will tell you—you don't need to blow your own horn; we must show humility. There are several schools not doing well academically and we must keep in mind where we used to be.

As a former high school basketball coach, I used to have my ball players recite this:

T—togetherness
E—effort
A—attitude
M—mental toughness—
Spells- TEAM—There is no I in the word TEAM.
TEAMWORK makes the DREAMWORKS!!

Confronting Challenges

Another challenge among urban high schools is teenage pregnancy. Admittedly, this is not a small issue; rather, it is a constant threat to disruption of an academic career. I have urged our female students not to trade their backpacks for diaper bags. I would visit the meetings that took place with our teenage parents. When local churches came in talking about abstinence, I wanted our school to be a part of that. The church would bring pink balloons into our school during lunch periods and the female students would sign up for a workshop or conference, with their mothers joining their daughters and encouraging them to wait before having sex. The name of the program was called Build-A-Wall. Since this program's inception, I honestly believe the number of female students giving birth declined at our school during the past five years. I constantly remind our students to make good choices and make good decisions!

Each morning in an urban school setting, we deal with students tardy to school. My assistant principal called me on my walkie-talkie and said, "Dr. Williams, I have a female student coming to see you because of excessive tardiness and she was upset about a pending suspension." When the student came into my office, she was visibly upset. She stated she had two babies and she was recently put out of the house prior to spring break. She was living with her boyfriend's parents. She was a senior with good grades. I called her mother on the phone and the student's story checked out, but she was adamantly clear that she wanted to complete her senior year. I instructed her whenever she was late again to enter through the main office door and I told my secretary to give her an excused admit and inform me if it became habitual. Well, in three months she walked across the stage and received her high school diploma. Even though there are many circumstances beyond our control and we can't save all of our students, this is a perfect example of the positive outcome we hope to achieve when we encounter situations with our students.

There was another student who was suspended for excessive tardiness. The student had been late thirteen times in one nine-week grading period. The parent was upset that the student was suspended for tardiness. I informed the parent that this overnight suspension is only a conference so we (parent/school) could detour this negative behavior. The parent said she brought the child to school every morning when she got off work. I told the parent that her child was failing her first-period class because she was missing assignments, and I said, "Mom, can you and I arrive to our job late every day without a negative consequence?" This mother and daughter needed to make it their priority for the student to be on time. We must have a plan. If we don't have a plan—we plan to fail.

Read this student's True Testimony:

Student's True Testimony

"I like this class because there is something different going on all the time.

My other class is like peanut butter for lunch everyday.

This class is like my teacher really knows how to cook.

It's like he owns a restaurant with a big menu and stuff."

Our scholars must enjoy learning. Learning should be fun and interesting!

Chapter 6: Educating Students of Today

The child's first teacher is their parent. But the second greatest influence on the student will be their teacher. Every classroom needs a great teacher. My instructional team and I made it our priority to hire great teachers. I would get a team of three or four teachers per academic discipline. I would set up interview teams based on those disciplines (i.e., English, math, and science teams). Those interview teams would select the top two candidates, and I would bring them back for a one-on-one interview with me as the instructional leader.

Great Teachers

The great teacher strives to be an equal partner with the parent and child in the educational process. The parents are always viewed as a positive element in a child's learning process, and the teacher tries to involve them in school activities whenever possible. This teacher is always very positive. Teaching, to such a person, is a mission based on the belief that every child can and will learn. The teacher provides individual students with the opportunity to learn by the use of a wide variety of learning materials and teaching styles. In fact, this teacher demands that students learn and will not be emotionally satisfied until every child demonstrates measureable progress. His or her classroom always holds a few surprises both for the administrator and the students, changes designed to transform the classroom atmosphere and stimulate learning. This is the teacher who maintains a constant dialogue with parents through notes, phone calls, and conferences. This is the great teacher.

TEACHER

The **MEDIOCRE** teacher **TELLS**

The **GOOD** teacher **EXPLAINS**

The **SUPERIOR** teacher **DEMONSTRATES**

The **GREAT** teacher **INSPIRES**

I always felt effective teachers motivate their students. They manage their classroom. They eliminate irresponsible student behavior. They implement differentiated instruction successfully. They model brain-compatible teaching and learning. They foster an emotionally engaging classroom, and they develop effective leadership strategies. Effective teachers do three things simultaneously: They demonstrate good teaching strategies, they come prepared with interventions for their students, and they model proactive discipline throughout the lesson if any student gets off track. Their universal philosophy might as well say: If you are always prepared you never need to spend time getting prepared. These are the same teachers who welcome administrators into their classrooms and they welcome classroom walk-throughs or unscheduled observations.

It is a known fact that most high-performing teachers leave high-performing schools because of poor climate. It is also a known fact that most high-performing teachers leave bad schools because they affect the teachers' overall Teacher Effectiveness Measure (TEM) scores. Hopefully, in the near future a happy medium can be found to ensure high performers are valued and appreciated no matter where they choose to work.

High-performing teachers provide their students multiple ways to engage content. There is a strong focus on teachers using engagement strategies that allow all students to practice, apply, and demonstrate content mastery through discussions and/or writing about complex text, tasks, or concepts. We are asking our teachers to talk less and prompt our students to talk more. As it relates to Common Core Standards, worksheets are used at a minimum.

Teacher-Student Ratio

I applaud any successful urban school with over 800 students. When your numbers are much larger, you have a tendency toward having students quit school or basically disappear, and no one misses them or knows they are gone. With the current focus on accountability regarding graduation rates, this is unacceptable. Also, I realize there are state laws relating to class sizes and teacher-to-student ratio.

But just imagine, as a coach you have ten, fifteen, to twenty players on a varsity team but you have assistant coaches to help plan, evaluate, strategize, and nurture the talent to their full potential. Imagine that on a football team composed of fifty to eighty players per team, you have three to five assistant coaches to help you do the things I mentioned earlier. So when it comes to educating our children in an urban school, you can have up to thirty-five students in a classroom, but without a second teacher (except in inclusive classrooms). How can you maximize the learning potential in that classroom if you have, let's say, three or four different learning styles? How can you differentiate instruction? How can you minimize distractions when students are learning at various levels? How difficult would it be to demonstrate content mastery in a classroom with a heterogeneous makeup of students?

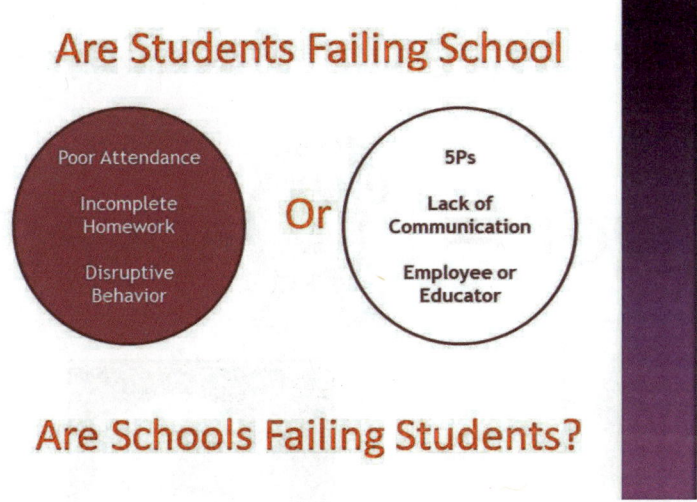

Figure 14

Effective Strategies

Figure 14 illustrates, are students failing schools or are schools failing students? As educators we must be honest with ourselves. We must provide timely interventions and multiple strategies to reach each and every child. We need hands-on manipulative and data-driven academic priorities. We aren't in the business of producing dropout factories. Dropout factories are defined as high schools with a graduation rate hovering around 55 percent. In some education institutions we have teachers failing over 50 percent of their students. I have worked at some schools where teachers had 70 percent of their classroom student population making Ds/Fs. Now, who is failing whom? That percentage is higher among African Americans. Another question could be asked: Why are a disproportionately number of our black boys referred to special education classes at a young age? Every black boy that's experiencing academic difficulty shouldn't be placed in special education. As Figure 15 shows, the only letter that moves our boys from ANGER TO DANGER is the letter D. We need trained and motivated professionals providing resources and effective strategies for our urban boys.

Figure 15

Disruptive behavior stains our schools. Sometimes it is the result of students not seeing a connection between the real world and the lesson being taught. To make lessons relevant, the following statements must be realized about our students of today:

They have a shorter attention span.
They are accustomed to being entertained.
They have remote controls in their heads.
They are mostly visual learners.
They are accustomed to receiving information faster than we are accustomed to giving it.

And yet despite these facts, great teachers make real world connections in their lesson delivery.

Figure 16 indicates what success looks like in the classroom.

SUCCESS
It must be a connection between

the real world

&

the lesson cemetery classroom?

Figure 16

They make learning fun and interesting. Students love going to their class. Some students run to get there. When they are out sick, the student makes sure their assignments are turned in. They will tell you, "I can't miss this class." There is a connection between reality and relevance.

Influence on Students

A significant challenge to educating students is the myriad of influences that impact their young lives. The next graph (Figure #17) depicts the greatest influence on students during specific decades. As you can see, the influence of home and church was less influential as we approached the turn of the century. Many of our students don't have morals or values in life. Home, school, and church don't have the same value as they did ten, twenty, and thirty years ago, hence the problems we are having today.

As the graph illustrates, if friends are the greatest influence on a student, and their influence is negative, it is easy to see how gangs became popular during the decades of the '80s and '90s. Whether we like it or not, educators must adapt to the learners of today.

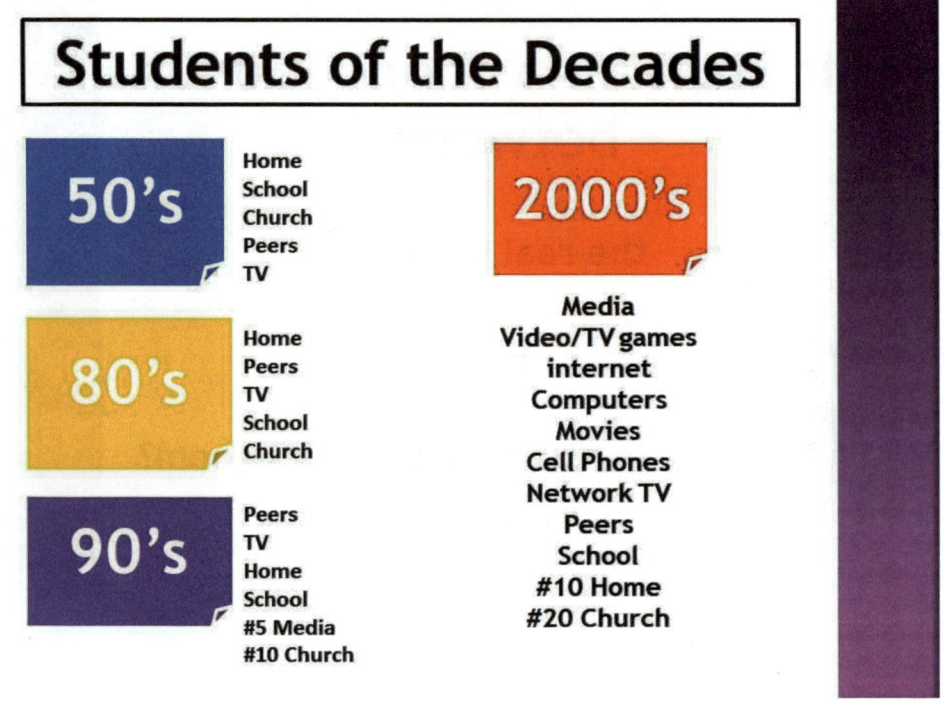

Figure 17

The graph also shows this century, with the greatest influences on our students being hands-on devices and technology. Our students are technologically savvy in the twenty-first century and our educators need to adjust accordingly. We must also make sure our students use technology in moderation. The cell phone can't become their oxygen supply. I have had students in my school take a suspension rather than surrender their cell phone and sadly, the parent often agrees to the same thing. If we have already taken the phone when the parent becomes involved, the parent may suggest, "Could you give the phone back to my child and he/she take the suspension?"

I also remember a student who came by the main office and asked the secretary if she could see me. I went and met the student briefly and asked her to come into my office and have a sit. She stated I took her phone in a classroom and asked if she could get it. I said, "No, not at this moment." With a straight face she stated, "I am not leaving your office until I get my phone." After I failed to convince her to leave, I summoned the officers to come by my office. They were shocked when I told them that this student refused to leave my office because I wouldn't give her her cell phone. They told her if she didn't leave this office she would be arrested. She said, "No, I am not leaving without my phone." They picked her up from the chair and she wrestled with them, knocking things off my desk and turning her chair over. They handcuffed her and she was transported downtown. Before I called her mom, I was thinking, wow, I have to tell a parent her child has been arrested for refusing to leave the principal's office because of a cell phone. When I contacted Mom, to my amazement, she wasn't surprise at her daughter's behavior and said she should have been arrested and expelled from school.

The Blame Game

When I was an assistant principal, I would tell my teachers, "You can tell kids between the ages of three to eight anything." Kids are very impressionable at that age. They believe in the Easter bunny, tooth fairy, and Santa Claus. Older children are a little bit savvy. Kids fourteen and up can tell if you genuinely care for them. They can look you right in your eye and tell if you are concerned about them and their well-being. If students know that you care, they will do anything for you to show you are appreciated as their teacher. They will give their best effort and do well on a quiz or project because they want you to succeed as a teacher and they want you to feel good or look good. On the flip side of it, and in their weird way of thinking, some students will refuse to take a test or do well because they feel they are hurting you as a teacher, which we all know is far from the truth.

Every successful urban educator should possess a gift of encouragement. It is free. A lot of people are just mean-spirited. We all have a human side. We should encourage our kids. Our kids love to play the blame game. It is my parents' fault. It's my teacher's fault. It's my stepparent's fault. It is my coaches' fault. They will blame anyone or everyone but themselves. I tell my students, "You don't pick your parents. You didn't ask to be here." I also tell my teachers, "You didn't choose your class schedule. You didn't pick your students. Sometimes during your teacher career, it's like playing cards: You may be dealt a bad hand or you may receive a challenging class. But as in a card game, you can't just throw the kids away for the semester and year. You must teach them, educate them, and move them academically."

During the school year and throughout this journey, every school should continue to sharpen its focus on the data to drive instruction and do so to effectively impact learning in the classroom. This includes ensuring there is a caring and highly competent teacher in every classroom and that our classrooms are consistent across the school campus with a standard of excellence.

In some educational circles, corporate America blamed the universities for graduating unprepared graduates for the workforce. Universities blamed high schools for not actually equipping scholars as they earned a high school diploma, and high schools blamed middle schools for their scholars' educational shortcomings. Middle schools blamed elementary schools for scholars not having a solid educational foundation, and elementary schools blamed the parents for not being the scholars' first teachers.

We used to tell our teachers to be sure to sweep in front of their classroom doorway first before they started to complain about others. If each teacher keeps their doorway clean, we will have a clean and pleasant school. If everyone on the street keeps their doorway clean, we will have a clean street, hence neighborhood, community, and eventually a clean city. These small efforts add up to larger positive accomplishments. But because the important smaller steps lay the foundation for larger ones, we celebrate the small successes. We want our teachers to be supported, inspired, and empowered.

Chapter 7: Tipping Points

TIPPING POINTS

DRESS CODE

CELL PHONE

INSUBORDINATION

FIGHTING

CLASS CUTTING

TARDIES

The last boss I had when I was an assistant principal was quite concerned about me leaving his school and taking on a challenge such as being a principal at a high profile school. He told the powers that be that I had the fortitude to handle this and if I was successful, I could write my ticket anywhere. But if I wasn't successful, he said I could be demoted back to an assistant principal for life. He was a very kind man and he cared for his administrative team and staff.

I learned a lot from him in a very short period of time. His greatest influence and unspoken philosophy to me was "The difference between stumbling blocks and stepping stones is how we use them." It wasn't what he said, it was his body language and what he practiced. No matter how many times he was hit with something negative or how long the day was, he would always come back the next day wired up and ready to go. That was contagious to me in a positive way. I didn't get a chance to dwell on the negative and that was a good thing before I moved on to my own school. Even though I worked there for "only" eighteen months, I could have stayed there for at least five years. He may disagree, but I believe I owe my success to him.

Identifying Infractions

In recalling lessons I learned during my early days as a new principal, I wouldn't advise others in this position to go into a building trying to fight everything that you want to change at once: bad teachers, bad students, bad community leaders, or bad parents. I took Malcolm Gladwell's book *The Tipping Point*, and I prioritized the top four, five, or six student discipline infractions. I felt I had to organize a team and come up with a plan and address the teachers' concerns at this urban school. If you remember in Chapter 2, under Result 3, I spoke about the index card where the teachers notated their concerns. I felt these six items gave our school the negative publicity that it received. These items were identified as the "Tipping Points."

When I arrived I pulled the discipline data and I noticed 88 percent of the referrals centered on six infractions. These top six "office referrals" may differ depending on what educational environment you are in. Our immediate concerns were:

- Dress code –students wearing various gang colors
- Class cutting—major consequences for repeated violators
- Tardiness—over 200-300 students late to school daily
- Cell phones—consistent consequences for visible phones and repeated offenders
- Insubordination—disrespecting adults in the building without severe consequences
- Fighting—consequences not severe enough, especially for repeaters

In this section, I will take a look at each of the six infractions and what we did to be consistent in giving out the negative consequences for those students who broke the rules. Teachers get upset, rightfully so, if the administration team isn't consistent with their consequences. I reinforced to our administrative team that we must get the parents involved and we must deal with chronic misbehavior through progressive discipline.

Early on during our administrative team's inception, students couldn't wear certain colored t-shirts, socks, even shoestrings, until we felt we had the gang colors under control. We expelled for gang graffiti displayed on folders, tablets, and personal backpacks. All dress code violators were immediately issued overnight suspensions as long as it didn't have gang overtones.

Class cutting and excessive tardiness received immediate consequences. Parents were contacted immediately and a conference held with the administrator. Progressive discipline was initiated. We knew these problems must be solved because chronic problems in these areas lead to truancy issues, long-term suspensions, and potential dropouts.

Cell phones and insubordination can be simultaneously linked together. When a student refused to give a phone to an adult (insubordination), it resulted in a three-day suspension. Insubordination is refusing to do what an adult says. We knew students had the phones. We didn't care as long as the phones were out of sight and we could not hear them. According to policy, insubordination suspensions could range from one to three days on the first offense.

I detest fighting. It is barbaric and savage behavior, though it is acceptable among many cultures. There were instances when I expelled ten students at the same time. There was another occasion when I expelled seventeen students for fighting on the way home. The logic was if you don't issue consequences for fighting immediately after school (30 minutes), that mess will permeate our school the next day. Sadly, some of our students mimic what they see their parents do. Fighting leads to bodily injuries that many times require medical treatment and transportation to the hospital. Early on during my principalship, I expelled every student thirty days or more for fighting. If the student had a history of fighting, I strongly suggested to pupil services that they should not return. And of course, social media has made fighting a YouTube sensation. Societal ills such as neighborhood conflicts, threats on social media, and irrational family members, if not monitored, can have explosive outcomes in your school.

We ran a behavior report after a semester and we were surprised at the results. I like to express these three categories as distinct colors. The colors were green, yellow, and red. Our green students represented 1,100 students who made good choices most of the time. They had no office referrals and no suspensions, with only an occasional tardy to school and/or class. This population made up nearly 80 percent of the student body.

Our next group made up 11-15 percent of the student population. This was the yellow group. Interventions needed to be placed on these students before they went down to red, or hopefully, improved to green. These students usually got suspended once per grading period. They were usually late to school and class, and we had to get the parents involved immediately. We issued overnight suspensions for infractions, which served as a parent conference. Progressive discipline was usually started on this group with the hope of improving the students' behavior. Progressive discipline ranged from a warning, detention, community service, or ISS for repeated infractions. Progressive discipline also could range from overnight, three-day, or five day suspensions, again, for repeat infractions.

Our last group was the red group. This group made up roughly 5-9 percent of the student population. These students were usually multiple violators of dress code, class cutting, excessive tardiness, and insubordination. Fighting usually resulted in a minimum of a ten-day suspension. Repeated violators for fighting would be immediately expelled. I even expelled students fighting on the way home. If I didn't issue consequences for violators on the way home, the issue would permeate our building the next day, disrupting the educational environment. Some principals wouldn't admit it, but students' safety on the way home is also of concern and if something occurred within thirty minutes of the students going home, I would deal with it the next day if it reached my desk. Students identified as the red group had parents with "frequent flyer" miles in our building. These students had a history of chronic negative behaviors. Some if not most of these students had been to an alternative school and placed back into the main population. Some of these parents eventually stopped coming to school to clear suspensions. This type of students eventually stops coming to school, and they are classified as high school dropouts.

Dropping Out

As it relates to dropouts, people who drop out of school are usually hanging around students who are exhibiting those negative behaviors, such as cutting class and skipping school. No student wakes up in the morning saying to themselves, "I am going to drop out today." Dropping out of school is a process. That process usually lasts several months, if not years.

I tell our students they should not hang with friends that have no purpose and that are not productive. I always reemphasize to them, "Show me your friends and I will show you your future."

One of society's flaws is that when something breaks out, we as a society run towards the problem. We tell our students if you run to trouble or run with a crowd, you never know what will greet you. The bullet or weapon of choice may strike you. I once heard we should not walk away from fools, we should run from them.

Early on I used to tell our students on the intercom, "Be Good or Be Gone," meaning if they didn't want to abide by the rules at school they would be gone. Students need to realize there are rules everywhere: rules at home, rules at school, rules on the job, there are even rules on the streets, and rules in jail. Most of our students' arrests that occurred during school hours were from incidents that happened off campus (weekends, holidays, after-school hours). When the detectives came to me and told me who they were looking for and why, I called the parents and let them know their son or daughter had been taken out the building in handcuffs because a warrant had been issued against them. I let the parents know I was just informing them as the principal. A few parents are outraged but most of them were not surprised. If the arrest was "per felony," we as an administrative team had to expel the student. Even though our community (after-school hours) had a bad repetition for foolishness, our school received several academic awards for achievement. Our administrative staff and teachers knew that happy students are productive students.

I wish we could have done a better job in recognizing those 1,100 students who exhibited good behavior. Administrative teams across this nation spend energy on negative behavior, and we need to come up with positive consequences for students who make good choices consistently.

When I was first appointed principal at this urban school, my administration team and I used to make surprise classroom visits. We would select two teams. Each team would consist of five members that included an officer, administrator, and coach. These classroom sweeps were predetermined by classroom rosters with highly volatile students, such as suspected gang members, high-profile negative behavior, or suspected drug sellers (based on student tips). We targeted certain classrooms in advance in different parts of the building because we knew students would try to text that we were doing surprise visits or, as they called them, drive-bys. The element of surprise made this very effective.

Using Tipping Points

We all have a tipping point in our lives. Since I was vertically challenged, I was always that last guy chosen on the basketball playground, but some guys picked me because of my hustle and desire and the fact that I hated to lose. I had to say, "Enough is enough!" I brought that same tenacity from the playground into my teenage years and adulthood. I was selected as Mr. Sophomore in high school. I was nominated and elected as Mr. Westwood during my senior year in high school. On a predominately white campus I was elected as secretary of communications in the Student Government Association.

A year later I was the first minority SGA president elected on the campus of the University of Tennessee at Martin. The historic win placed me in *Jet* and *Ebony* magazines. I received 49.6 percent of the vote while my white male opponent received 47 percent of the vote. The next year I was elected to a second term by a much wider margin while campaigning against two different opponents. The second win is always tougher because now you are not running on promises you made before your first term but what you actually accomplished during the first term.

After graduating from college, in my first interim teaching assignment, I was the third teacher in this particular classroom in one year. The former teacher had severe classroom management and discipline issues. That teacher was a 6'3" burly guy who couldn't handle the classroom. When I was selected as an interim teacher in the month of November, people said I wasn't going to last. At the end of the year, I was hired as a full-time teacher at my high school alma mater, where I stayed three years. Even though that was twenty-five years ago, that is why today, I have zero tolerance for any teacher who can't manage their classroom.

Later on I went to another school to teach and coach a sport that I had never played before. People said I wasn't going to be successful. Two years later, that junior high team was crowned district champ and runner-up in a city championship game. When I moved to high school coaching, they said the kids loved me but I would not be successful. I must admit I used unorthodox methods in reaching my basketball players. There was one game in particular that became really intense. I felt I wasn't getting the best out of one of my players. He stood 6'8" and the gym was loud. I yelled his name and motioned him to run to me. When he got to me I stood up in a chair and looked him eye-to-eye and gave him stern instructions.

I was one of those coaches who didn't like to blame officials for our shortcomings. I would tell my players, "YOU decide the outcome!" Motivating my players during pregame, halftime, and postgame rhetoric was the norm. Well, nine years later my teams played in six district tournament finals, three regional finals, and a state tournament appearance. The hustle and desire to win and the fact that I hated to lose stayed with me. I worked harder than the average person.

As I went into administration, the naysayers said I would not be successful, especially in an urban school. Needless to say, they didn't realize I had an urban school pedigree. I took the same tenacity into administration that I'd had as a teacher and coach. When I told my players don't blame the outcome of the game on the referees, the same applied when I told my teachers don't blame the outcome on our kids' background. You know what environment you are working in. You know where our kids are from. For the most part, you chose this environment. Let's not enable our students or make excuses for them. We must push and challenge them. I asked my teachers to teach out of their comfort zone, especially when they were introducing a new lesson or trying to motivate their students. In some subject areas or content, you need to do something creative to drive home a point or make learning relevant.

This brings me to another unorthodox technique. A few of my teachers knew I used to dance back in the day. For a motivational skit at our Gateway or EOC pep rally, they asked me to perform before the student body. After some soul searching, I did as my teachers asked and I was surprised at the nearly 300 electronic devices that appeared from teachers, staff, and even the student body. They sat there quietly as I danced, recording the performance with their cell phones and iPads. That was truly out of my confront zone. Every now and then, it's ok for our students to see us in a different light. Furthermore, I received several phone calls from parents who said they wished they had been there and they remembered my performing back in the day.

Finally, I didn't let people define me. Our destiny is not written *for us*; it's written *by us*, or we can say your destiny isn't determined for you –in all actuality, it's determined by you.

Another tipping point is not allowing negative situations to snowball into larger situations. As an effective school administrator, you can't sweep problems under the rug and think they will not resurface, or "tip," thus the name tipping point. Here are a few situations I would like for you to ponder and think how you would deal with these real-time events.

1. You have just been notified by a confident source that a social media Web site states there will be a student walkout during lunch. How would you address this issue?

2. A disgruntled parent is unhappy about the decisions you have made as a principal. She has taken it upon herself to picket her dissatisfaction of you as the school leader. She is holding a sign on the sidewalk before school starts and during school's dismissal. She is trying to rally other parents for her cause. How would you address this issue?

3. A teacher walks into your office after being absent for three days without calling in, which constituents a "no call-no show." The teacher arrives back to school on the fourth day and tells you he or she was kidnapped. How would you address this issue?

4. It has come to your attention that a petition is being circulated by someone at your school indicating their dissatisfaction of your job performance. How would you address this situation without offending the teachers and staff who support you?

5. You must have a conversation with a difficult parent. Her child has been suspended several times in the past. The information that you have suggests that her child has feelings towards another student of the same sex. Without stating the obvious and without uttering the word *homosexual*, how would you handle that conference?

6. You just received a called from an irate parent who says that her child didn't come home last night. The parent said her son was arrested while at school the day before and she wasn't notified. She is headed to the school, she wants heads to roll, and she wants to see you (as the principal). How would you conduct this conference?

I have faced each of these situations or some very near to them. When addressing each one, I had to decide what my tipping points were and then respond accordingly. Not only that, but I had to decide in advance. There is no time to adequately prepare when the crisis is upon you. You must know your tipping points in advance and be prepared to have "courageous" conversations with difficult teachers, staff, alumni, parents, board members, stakeholders, and constituents alike when circumstances call for it.

Chapter 8: Conclusion

Be Good or Be Gone

Our urban school students encounter tragedies, traumas, addictions, abuse, and personal victimizations. Our students today face ambiguities that adults usually encounter. Our students are carrying a lot of emotional baggage. But on the other end of the spectrum, a lot of our young people lack morals. The language that comes out of their mouths in the hallway, cafeteria, and sometimes in the classrooms is learned. No one is born using bad language. No one is born prejudiced. That behavior is learned. No one is born to hate or love. That behavior has to be taught or learned. Some of our students don't even fear the police. The reasons some students give for being involved in fighting are sickening, "I just don't like him or her," "I don't like their friends," "I just want to fight them," or "They were mean mugging me" (slang for staring at someone or somebody). We expelled over 120 students in a 3-year period. With social media, I honestly think it will get worse before it gets better.

In some communities, violence among adults is an acceptable way to resolve disputes. Our children who witness this behavior grow up thinking that it is the normal way to deal with conflict. There you have it: a conflict at school involving two students, and when their parents arrive, you have a larger mess. A combination of bad or poor parenting and/or the combination of bad or poor communities will eventually lead to bad and troubled schools. The school is only a microcosm of the community. Don't misunderstand me, some schools are good schools in spite of the environment from which their students come, but it isn't the norm. In other words, there are many schools nationwide that perform well academically in spite of their environment. But it takes special administrative staff, teachers, and especially concerned and involved parents to incorporate those values and morals into those students to make that school rise beyond expectations. That's why a certain segment of our community is tired of violence in their urban schools and many of our parents are looking at other educational options for their children.

I have read an article entitled "School House to Jail House." I personally thought about the challenges of changing the cradle to prison pipeline video to cradle to college or cradle to career. Our older students need options. We must expose them to as many things as possible. When my own children were younger, I told them what to do. They didn't have options. Now as high school and college students they have options, and when they call me, I only provide advice. But since that vehicle was put in place many years ago, the choices they make are usually well grounded. Yes, they still will make mistakes, but hopefully (at this point) they will not be career-shattering mistakes.

Education and Income

Every parent wants their child to go farther or obtain a better education than themselves. All of our students in urban high schools will not attend college, but as the following graph projects, the more education you obtain, the higher your income will be.

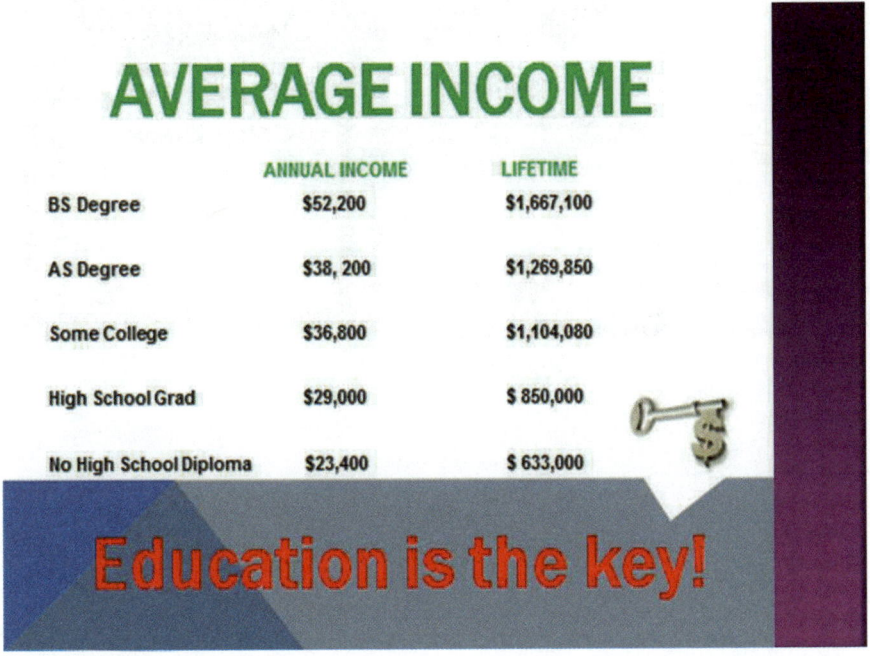

AVERAGE INCOME

	ANNUAL INCOME	LIFETIME
BS Degree	$52,200	$1,667,100
AS Degree	$38, 200	$1,269,850
Some College	$36,800	$1,104,080
High School Grad	$29,000	$ 850,000
No High School Diploma	$23,400	$ 633,000

Education is the key!

To realize their fullest potential, students must apply and invest themselves while in school by working hard. Then they can "play" later when they begin to reap the rewards of their hard work. Life is going to be hard no matter what route or path you take. But the journey will be a little easier if you take school seriously while you are younger. Do the work early and it will pay off later.

WORK First as a student—Studying; completing homework assignments; utilizing the five Ps—Proper Planning Prevents Poor Performance; navigating successfully through SAT, ACT, college entry and exit exams, and comps.

PLAY later as an adult—Savings; vacations; traveling; shopping; investments; and enjoying better health.

That is why I have coined the phrase "Work first vs. Play later or Play first vs. Work harder later." I have brought about open debate on this conversation at several speaking engagements in churches, open houses, and PTSA functions. Students can either work now and play later, or they can play while in school, and work harder later to catch up.

PLAY first as a student—Poor attendance; excessive tardiness; class cutting; truancy, poor grades; suspensions, juvenile court visits, poor educational habits; and potential dropout.

WORK harder as an adult—Night school; GED programs; obtaining additional certifications; inconsistent in keeping a job; working two or three jobs simultaneously, dealing with challenges to get better health benefits, poor health, and government assistance.

The Sum of Experiences

Students bring to school a sum of their life experiences. After all, life is composed of the sum of our choices. Perhaps Maya Angelou put it best in these words: "You are the sum total of everything you've ever seen, heard, eaten, smelled, been told, forgot – it's all there. Everything influences each of us, and because of that I try to make sure that my experiences are positive."

Some students and families I have taught, coached, or served have excelled in spite of their negative experiences. My hat is off to them. Because of them, I was truly inspired.

But negative influences remain a challenge. All schools weren't created equally. Our public schools are becoming a more of a challenge. Parents have more options than ever before concerning where to send their most important prized possession—their child. But with the breakdown of neighborhoods, communities, and even homes and families, the neighborhood and community schools will ultimately suffer the consequences. On the other hand, even though times have changed, even though we are living in a new era, no one cares where you live, no one cares where your school is located, and no one cares about the teachers and administrators who are assigned or selected to work within that school, the bottom line is RESULTS. Everyone is expecting RESULTS. Are your teachers and administrators effective and are your students moving up that trajectory?

Recently, I read an article in the Memphis, Tennessee, newspaper, *Commercial Appeal*. The article, entitled "Wired to Win," said sociologists referred to a particular group of students as "high-achieving, low-income." Too often, these are the students who don't get enough help. Fewer than 1 in 10 high-achieving, low-income students even apply to the more selective colleges their wealthier peers attend. "They assume they can't afford it so don't even bother to apply," said Jae Henderson, a Memphis native and author who founded an organization called College Bound to address the problem. It's a phenomenon known as "undermatching," which contributes to the country's widening income inequality.

According to a White House report issued earlier this year, the share of jobs that require postsecondary education has doubled over the last forty years. When children born into the bottom fifth of the income distribution get a college degree, their chances of making it to the top nearly quadruple. And their chances of making it out of the bottom increase by more than 50 percent.

"Low-income students often lack the guidance and support they need to prepare for college, apply to the best-fit schools, apply for financial aid, enroll and persist in their studies, and ultimately graduate," the White House report noted. "As a result, large gaps remain in educational achievement between students from low-income families and their high-income peers." In the near foreseeable future, our school counselors need to be trained and assessable to help our disadvantage students.

Recently, in my hometown in Memphis, Tennessee, our Shelby County Board of Education has launched broad and bold initiative. The initiative is called 80/90/100. This initiative will support what the White House report is saying. Its goals were established to ensure that by the year 2025, 80 percent of Shelby County School's students will be career and college ready, 90 percent of students will graduate from high school, and 100 percent of students who graduate will enroll in a postsecondary learning opportunity.

"These are very ambitious goals for our students, but I firmly believe they are attainable with the right strategic vision and plan,"

Superintendent Dorsey Hopson stated. "I am thankful that Board members share my enthusiasm and optimism and recognize the tremendous impact this can have on our community at large." By setting clear goals and targets, Shelby County Schools can be transparent and accountable to the community, align funding with strategies that have the greatest possible impact, and consistently communicate success and failures. "Today's global economy demands that students be college or workforce ready," Hopson said.

As an administrator, I was truly blessed in being prepared to deal with struggles of our community due to my own family struggles and my own self-induced personal struggles. When I was in elementary school my dad was incarcerated for nearly ten years basically for circumstantial evidence in a deadly robbery. That left my mom providing for me and my sister alone at an early age. Struggles that I saw my mother go through and my struggles in early adulthood that were self-induced such as bad relationships and child support gave me another perspective so that I was able to connect with many parents who came through my office. The fundamental breakdown of families and the term *blended families* were dynamics that I used to have healthy discussions for the betterment and success of their child. The best advice came from my mom in my early adulthood. She stated, "If you don't forgive your father for not being around when you were a child, you can't become a good father yourself someday." I didn't know what that phrase meant but "boy" it came into perspective as I got older and wiser.

In this business of education, urban school administrators come and go. You can either come after an effective administrator or one that wasn't that effective. All across this nation many urban administrators have sight and many have vision. But if you have an administrator that has sight but no vision, you will be able to tell because their conversation will be flawed. They will spend time talking negatively about the past and forget the shoulders of individuals they rode who either assisted or trained them for their current position. They pretend they have all the answers. They will isolate themselves on an island. They will have the tendency to use the pronoun "my" program instead of "our" program. But on the other hand, if they possess sight and vision, you also can tell that in their conversation. They will call the names of individuals who got them to where they are, and they will have a keen sight on how to improve from those past successes. Furthermore, if mistakes were made in the past, they will have crystal clear vision about correcting the errors without placing blame on their predecessors or teachers. This urban school principalship is no joke. We must be humble and appreciative because we are only there for a short time.

In closing this book, and with respect for its title, I would like to offer one final thought: Throughout all obstacles urban school administrators encounter and the trials and tribulations we encounter, if you can show me urban school educational leaders that possess these seven qualities along with the ability to tackle these obstacles, I will show you a school that any teacher would love to work in along with a principal that a teacher would love to work for.

*Yours in Education,   **RRW***

Shelby County Schools

State Recognizes 39 SCS Schools as Reward Schools for Top
Achievement or Growth

(2008)
Kirby High School
High Priority
to

(2014)
Kirby High School
REWARD SCHOOL

Appendix—Background

After a twenty-five-year career, I accepted a new challenge. However, the new school was soon closed due to low enrollment, so now I find myself at a crossroads, but eagerly looking for a new opportunity in which to apply the principles that I have found to be effective. I must admit I am a little nervous about my future, but I am very excited about this book before it goes to publication. I recently remembered a quote: "Happiness can be found even in the darkest of times, if one remembers to turn on the light." I am presently looking for the switch.

Pictures of Former Schools

KIRBY HIGH SCHOOL

Memphis, Tennessee

2006-2014

CENTRAL HIGH SCHOOL

Memphis, Tennessee

2004-2006

SOUTHWIND MIDDLE SCHOOL

Memphis, Tennessee

2004

ELMORE PARK MIDDLE SCHOOL

Bartlett, Tennessee

2003

BOLTON HIGH SCHOOL

Arlington, Tennessee

1993-2003

VANCE MIDDLE SCHOOL

Memphis, Tennessee

1990-1993

WESTWOOD HIGH SCHOOL

Memphis, Tennessee

1986-1990

My Background

Memphis teacher receives recognition

Reginald Williams, grandson of Mr. and Mrs. E.R. Brown of Magnolia, was recently recognized for his accomplishments.

Williams attended the University of Tennessee at Martin, Tenn. He completed a double major and received a B.S. degree in Geo-Science and Physics on June 18, 1985.

While in college, Williams was the first black to be elected as president of the Student Government in 1983 and the first to serve two terms in 25 years. A notice of his election appeared in *Jet, Ebony* , and *The Commercial Appeal*. He met many famous people, but the few who stand out are Mayor Andrew Young; Lorene Bennett Jr., *Ebony* advisor; Ned McWherter, who is now governor of Tennessee; and Charles Smith, who is Commissioner of Education for the State of Tennessee. "I guess this proved to be very special and most meaningful of times for me...", he said.

Williams is the recipient of the American Legion Award, F.G. Calvin Leadership Award; the Raeer Award, and the Distinguished Young Leadership Award. He has been named Distinguished Collegian of the Year, Tennessee College Brother of the Year, and a member of Who's Who Among Students in American Universities. He received all three twice.

Reginald Williams

1984-85. He has also received the Outstanding Young Men of America Award three times. Mr. Williams said, "Looking back on my college years, I must truly say my greatest asset was that I was able to communicate effectively with a cross-section of individuals. That was definitely a God-given talent."

After leaving UT-Martin, he had several job interviews before deciding to teach. Job offers in Cleveland and Boulder, Colo., didn't interest him. He said, "If something else came along I would definitely consider it. You always want to better yourself, no matter what you are doing. Teaching is a respected profession; it's going to get its due respect. (If not, industries will get them.)" Williams feels that there are three basic beliefs that are essential to success; believe in yourself, have a sense of direction where you are going, and believe in God.

His future goals are to continue his education where he has an interest - in higher education - and help as many youngsters as possible.

Williams is currently teaching at his own alma mater, Westwood High School in Memphis, Tenn.

SPORTS

e Defender, Saturday, May 31 - June 4, 2003, Page **6B**

Bolton roasts Coach Williams

Williams

by Bill Little
Tri-State Defender Sports Editor

He can't leap tall buildings in a single bound nor can he travel faster than a speeding bullet, but Reginald is the epitome of high energy. Reginald Williams has an abnormal metabolic rate.

I'm not talking about someone who is six feet plus, and weighs over 200 pounds. Williams, who just concluded his ninth year as head basketball coach at Bolton High School is closer to five feet tall than six feet, and his weight is closer to 150 pounds than 200.

A task master, despite his diminutive stature, Williams has a career move to make and basketball coaching isn't in the picture. Williams,   realizes that he is going to reach a life-long dream of getting his doctorate, and becoming a school administrator, the window of opportunity is closing in on him.

After nine winning seasons at Bolton Williams may be moving on soon.

Williams is so appreciated at Bolton it appears the Shelby County School has taken him for granted.

Coach Williams was roasted on

May 17th at Bolton in appreciation for his outstanding services. The Wildcats made it to the regional quarterfinals last season while compiling a 19-11 record.

Williams also would like to spent more time with his wife Tina, sons Jeremy (8), Reginald Jr. (9) and daughter Lakecia. The long and arduous grind of the coaching season and nearly 40 miles of daily driving from Memphis to Arlington, Tenn. and back is time consuming.

Williams has spend teaching and coaching assignments at Westwood High and Vance Jr. High before moving to Bolton seeking a fresh start in the Shelby County School system.

Athletics isn't the first thing that gained notoriety for Williams. He headed up a popular dance group known as the Aces while a teacher at Westwood. The fast-paced group performed at half-time of basketball and other school functions.

A graduate of UT Martin, Williams was known for his academic prowess. However, his mother Mae C. Williams, taught Physical Education in the Memphis City Schools and father Willie Williams played quarterback for Tuskegee Institute in the 1960s.

"GET YOUR HEAD IN THE GAME"

14 Things That Matter Most

1. Great teachers never forget that it is people, not programs, that determine the quality of a school.

    - If a school has great teachers, it is a great school
    - If my child has a great teacher, I see the school as great
    - We spend a great deal of time looking for programs that will solve our problems
    - It is relationships (people) that matter the most

2. Great teachers establish clear expectations at the start of the school year and follow them consistently as the year progresses.

    - Great teachers have expectations, not rules
    - Set expectations and then establish relationships so that students want to meet these expectations.
    - Great teachers expect good behavior, and they generally get it.

3. When a student misbehaves, great teachers have one goal: to keep that behavior from happening again.

    - Great teachers are motivated to prevent misbehavior.
    - Ineffective teachers are motivated to punish the student.
    - When a student has to be referred to the office, an effective teacher wants students to be better when they leave the office, not angry.

- Ineffective teachers want students angry and angry students are a problem.

   Example: (Nothing happened)

- Treat students with respect
- Treat their parents with respect no matter how they act.

4. Great teachers have high expectations for students but even higher expectations for themselves.

5. Who is the variable in the classroom?

   - Great teachers know that they are the variable.
   - Great teachers consistently strive to improve and focus on something that they control- themselves
   - All teachers have expectations for students
   - Ineffective teachers expect students to be engaged no matter how irrelevant or boring their material is that day. They expect students to pay attention no matter how boring they are.
   - GREAT TEACHERS HAVE HIGH EXPECTATIONS FOR STUDENTS, BUT HAVE HIGHER EXPECTATIONS FOR THEMSELVES.
   - Example: What if you give a test and all of the students do poorly, whom does he/she blame? An ineffective teacher blames the students, parents, administration, MTV, drugs, gangs, etc. A great teacher accepts responsibility for their classrooms!
   - What behavior can you control? Your own!

6. **Great teachers create a positive atmosphere in their classroom and their schools.**

- They treat everyone with respect
- They understand the power of praise
- Ten out of ten
- You do not have to like students, but you have to act like you do.
- Do great teachers like some of their students less than others? Of course they do!
- Whether they like the students or not they act like they do.

POWER OF PRAISE

Authentic praise- praise for something genuine

Specific praise- the behavior we praise will probably be repeated.

Immediate praise

Praise must be clean- do not praise to get students to do something in the future, and do not use "but" in the praise.

Praise must be private

7. **Great teachers constantly filter out the negatives that do not matter and share the positive attitude.**
   - **If a student hears us whining, it will be the talk of the school for days.**
   - **When a teacher sneezes, the whole class catches a cold.**
   - **"This is the worst group of kids we've ever had."**
   - **"They only care about their kids."**
   - **Perception is reality!**

8. **Great teachers work hard to keep their relationships in good repair to avoid personal hurt and to repair possible damage.   Example: Johnny**

9. **Great teachers have the ability to ignore trivial disturbances and the ability to respond to inappropriate behavior without escalating the situation.**

10. **Great teachers have a plan for everything they do. If things do not work out they reflect on what they could have done differently and adjust their plans accordingly.**

11. **Before making any decision or attempting to bring about any change, great teachers ask themselves: What will the best people think? Many great students will be fine no matter what you decide, but they will no longer be great.**

12. **Great teachers constantly ask themselves who is most comfortable and who is least comfortable with the decisions they make. They treat everyone as if they are good.**

13. Great teachers keep standardized testing in perspective. They focus on the real thing- student learning.

14. Great teachers care about their students. They understand that behaviors and beliefs are tied to emotion, and they understand the power of emotion to jump-start change.

DEBORAH DAVIS, 11:55 AM 10/25/99, Guest Speaker - Reggie William

```
Date: Mon, 25 Oct 1999 11:55:01 -0500
Reply-To: debdavis@utm.edu
Sender: owner-campus-1@utm.edu
From: DEBORAH DAVIS <debdavis@utm.edu>
To: campus-1@utm.edu
Subject: Guest Speaker - Reggie Williams
X-Sender: debdavis@mailer.UTM.edu
X-Mailer: QUALCOMM Windows Eudora Light Version 3.0.5 (32)
```

Today! Monday, October 25th @ 4 p.m. in Room 229 of the UC, Mr. Reggie R. Williams, will be the guest speaker for the Harold Conner Recipients. We would like to invite any UTM faculty and staff to attend.

Reggie Williams graduated from UTM in June of 1985. Received his Master's Degree in Administration & Supervision from Trevecca Nazarene College in 1989. While at UTM he served (2) terms as president of the Student Government Assoication. He will also be remembered by Mu Beta Chapter of Alpha Phi Alpha Fraternity for leading the brothers to (2) consecutive state, regional, and national championships in stepping. He was also named Tennessee College Brother of the Year twice. After leaving UTM, he continue to give exemplary service by being hired by the Memphis City Schools System. He was a teacher and coach at Westwood High School and Vance Deregulated Jr. High School. He was an energetic and dedicated teacher at both schools.

"Little Reggie" (a name given to him at UTM), became "Big Reggie" after stepping into the footsteps of legendary Bolton Coach Joe Branch. As Assistant basketball coach in 1993, he helped lead Bolton to the TSSAA state quarterfinals in basketball.
In 1994, Reggie was named head coach and led his team to an amazing 25-8 record. His team was League Champions & District Runner-up. He was again named Coach of the Year in the District.
Deborah Davis
Office of Student Affairs
223 Administration Bldg.
Martin, TN 38238

(901)587-7703
Fax: (901)587-7708
debdavis@utm.edu

THE COMMERCIAL APPEAL

Monday, July 21, 2003

Bolton basketball coach moving on

By Jim Masilak

masilak@gomemphis.com

Twice Reginald Williams had been offered the chance to move into school administration, and twice the Bolton High boys basketball coach had declined.

However, when Williams was offered a job as an assistant principal at Elmore Park Middle School, the lure proved too strong.

"I said no in 1997 because I wanted to continue to coach. They came to me in 2000 and I said no again," Williams said. "This time I thought it was the right time. If you keep saying no, eventually they'll quit knocking."

Williams, 39, stepped down after nine years at Bolton, including eight as the Wildcats' head coach, to accept a job nearer to his Southeast Memphis home.

"I've been doing 60-mile round trips about 200 times for about 10 years," said Williams, who often slept in the locker room at Bolton following road games. "This is a chance of a lifetime, and I couldn't pass it up."

Williams, who previously coached at Westwood High and Vance Middle, compiled a 190-106 record at Bolton. His Wildcat teams finished either first or second in their district in seven of his eight seasons.

The diminutive Williams, a UT-Martin graduate, never played basketball at a high level. "But my kids always played hard for me," he said. "That made up for the things I didn't know."

Bolton athletic director Chad Stevens said Williams would be missed.

"You can't say there's anyone who was more dedicated to a program than he was," Stevens said. "During basketball season, he lived (at the school). He put forth everything he had for the program."

Shelby County Schools is searching for a candidate to replace Williams. For details, visit the SCS Web site at *www.scs.k12.tn.us.*

3. East Shelby Review,

Bolton High Teacher Has Seen It All

by Rhonda K. Wilson

One adjective Reginald Williams, a local teacher, probably would not use to describe himself is unseasoned. That is because personally and professionally, he has tried to see it all.

Williams started teaching physical science at Bolton High School this school year, 1993-1994. He also is the head coach of the freshmen boys basketball team, the junior varsity boys basketball team and the girls track team and the assistant coach of the varsity boys basketball team. What a load, one might say. But Williams said he believes he has learned more as a teacher because of the different mix of students he has taught throughout his career.

Williams' first teaching job was at Westwood High School, his alma mater. Westwood is near Whitehaven in Southwest Memphis. There, Williams taught English, science and math and coached the varsity girls volleyball and softball teams and the junior high boys basketball team.

Four years later, Williams moved to Vance Junior High School in Midtown, "one of the toughest schools in Memphis," he said. At Vance, which is surrounded by four housing projects, Williams taught math and coached the boys basketball team, leading the players to the city championship last year. But after four years at Vance, Williams decided he wanted to teach at Bolton, a county school, because he had accomplished everything he could at the other schools, he said.

"As we approach the 21st century, to be a well-diversified educator you need to teach all types of students," Williams said, "from the lower socioeconomic status to the upper socioeconomic status, from the urban area to the rural area, from junior high to senior high."

Williams said at both Westwood

and Vance, all of the students are black compared to about 13 percent black students at Bolton. And 95 percent of the students at Vance are on the free-lunch program.

In one of Williams' eighth grade classes at Vance, eight of his students were mothers and at least four were 16 or older, he said.

"It's mind-boggling to me to see a (Bolton) teacher complain that they have one or two bad apples when at Vance I had nine bad apples in each class period," he said.

Williams said he is glad he has had the chance to work with a variety of students.

"All kids are basically the same, no matter the size, color, school system or whatever," he said. "Their needs may be different.

"The kids (at Bolton) are concerned with getting a car at 16. The kids at Westwood were concerned more about fashion. Vance was a different sector where those kids were more concerned about what they're gonna eat the next day, trying to find clean clothes to wear and being able to get a good night's sleep without hearing gunshots and the threat of drugs and violence in their neighborhood," he said.

Bolton uses internal suspension for disciplinary purposes, and Williams said he believes it is effective at Bolton. But that alone would not work at all schools, he said. Instead, students with severe disciplinary problems should be sent to an alternative school for troubled youths, he said.

In the last 10 years, Williams has won more than 30 local, state and national awards for coaching, teaching and civic duties.

While Williams' teaching career has taken him many places in Memphis, his college career afforded him the opportunity to travel throughout

the United States.

Williams, originally from Memphis, majored in GEO science and physics at the University of Tennessee at Martin. There, he became the first, and so far the only, minority student government president at UT Martin. In a college that was 11 percent black, he was elected to this office twice. This position allowed him to travel to 35 states and meet many kinds of people, he said. He also became a member of Alpha-Phi-Alpha fraternity.

Williams later decided he wanted to become certified to teach, which is common in his family. His mother, grandmother and aunt all taught school. He also received a master's degree in administration supervision and is now 10 classes short of a phD.

For fun, Williams, who is single, likes to watch television, read and socialize with his friends. He enjoys spending weekends entertaining his 3-year-old daughter in his East Memphis home and he is an active member of Pilgrim Rest Baptist Church.

Williams plans to get his doctorate some day and would like to go into administration. He said he generally likes to stay at one school no more than four or five years or until he feels like he has done all that he can there. People need to change and move on if they are no longer growing where they are, he said.

The doors probably will be open for Williams to teach anywhere because of his experience in a wide variety of teaching environments.

"I can definitely say if I decide to leave Bolton some day, I have a well diversified background," he said.

REGINALD R WILLIAMS

From:	JENNIFER M RUCKER
Sent:	Monday, February 24, 2014 5:04 PM
To:	REGINALD R WILLIAMS
Subject:	:(

Dr. Williams,

Let me first thank you for the opportunity to even come aboard the Kirby High School team. Truly it has been among the greatest of my teaching experiences to date. And then let me thank you for seeing enough potential in me to foster the development of my leadership skills within this building. Though the learning coach position was not one I sought out, and is often incredibly demanding, I will say that it is helping me reflect on and hone my own craft as an educator and I thank you for that. Most of all though, I'd like to thank you for your impeccable character. Thank you for leading with your heart and not your ego. Thank you for caring about your teachers and our students. Thank you for your humor and your passion. There's a very clear reason that you garner the respect that you do from both your staff and your students--you care about us all, and it's obvious. Believe me, that's no small thing. I think we've all been around long enough to have the misfortune of working with or for people who abuse positions of authority. Thank you for not being one of them. I'm sad to see you go, because it's truly been a pleasure to work for you. I appreciate your fairness, your candor when we need to be put in check, your willingness to hear and heed our opinions when appropriate, and your belief in and appreciation of all of us. These qualities in a leader are desired, but rarely found. I know you'll leave us in good hands, but there'll never be another you. Believe me, every second has been a pleasure. Thank you from the bottom of my heart for daily teaching us all what leading with compassion looks like. May a wealth of blessings follow you into your next venture. You do indeed deserve them.

Much love,
Rucker-Leake

THIS IS WHY I AM PROUD OF YOU!

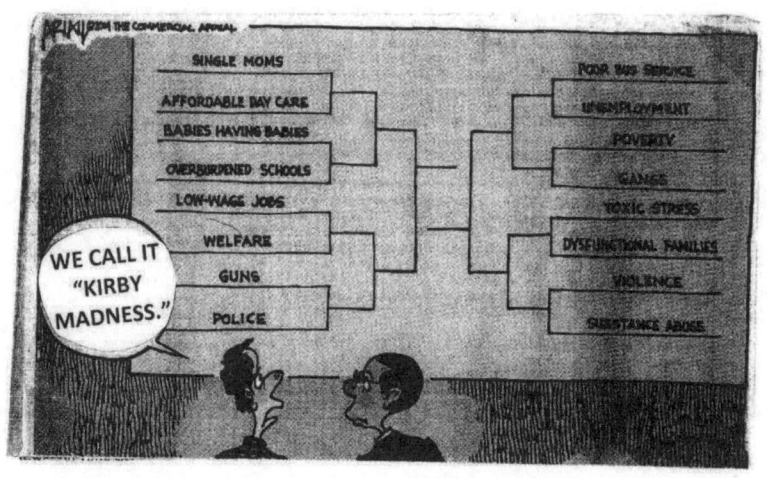

**LET'S KEEP PUSHING! LET'S KEEP REACHING!
NO EXCUSES, JUST RESULTS!**

Superintendent of Schools
Kriner Cash, Ed.D.

Office of the Superintendent
Breakthrough Leadership. Breakthrough Results.

July 27, 2009

Mr. Reginald Williams
Kirby High School
4080 Kirby Parkway
Memphis, TN 38115

Dear Mr. Williams:

I write with congratulations, first, to you on your leadership, and on your school's recent achievements on the state tests and with the Adequate Yearly Progress (AYP) release of last week. After reviewing the data from across the district, it is clear that your team did a great job during the 2008-09 school year. Please let your staff and students know how much I appreciate their hard work and dedication to academic achievement.

As we go forward into the new school year, I encourage you and your team to strive for even higher goals and ensure that all students are receiving the best education possible. While state tests are only a part of the educational context, we know that the stakes get higher and the expectations more rigorous this year. I am confident that you and your team are up to the challenge; our students deserve nothing less than our very best. Again, congratulations!

Sincerely,

Kriner Cash, Ed. D.
Superintendent

Memphis Commercial Appeal Newspaper

Wednesday, March 18, 2009

Letter to the Editor

Kirby principal blazes path to glory

I have had many occasions to interact with the Kirby High School teachers and principal. In every case, I have had the satisfaction of knowing that the educators there are responsive to students and parents.

Therefore, it was no surprise to me to see in The Commercial Appeal March 13 that Kirby has been honored as one of the five Gold-Gain Schools. I attribute this to the direction of the principal, Reginald Williams. His enthusiasm and passion for his school and students are obviously contagious.

RAY SCHWARTZ
Memphis

 # THAT CHILD IS ME

I don't live in TV land where things are always great.
I live in the projects surrounded by hate.
I live with my grandmother, since my mother left.
And it's my responsibility to do better for myself.
I live with people in my neighborhood, who abuse life,
  who are up to not good.
I live near where the houses are old and run down.
And we continue the destruction in our part of town.
I live with mice and the roaches roam.
They're my constant companions when I'm at home.
I live in frustration.
Discontent is my friend.
I wonder if this life will ever end.
At school I'm ignored.
I don't have nice clothes.
And the ones that I have are sometimes dirty, with holes.
Sometimes the only meal I eat is at school.
My only mask is acting real cool.
But I'm hungry, frustrated, at home there's no relief.
So I escape to a fantasy - to outrun my grief.
For I have to see something on which to wish and dream.
Then my life won't be hopeless, or as bad as it seems.
I have to find sanity, in my insane way,
Or I'd lose the battle, my soul would run away.
Don't judge without understanding, don't retreat without a fight.
But trusting you is something I've been taught I have no right.
The few who've shown concern, saw my stripes and fled.
The loss of hope cut so deep, that my spirit ached and bled.
But if you keep reaching and won't back down.
If you gain my trust, and stay around.
If you can love me dirty, nasty, clean, no manners, no training,
  just a broken dream.
If you can just look at what I could be,
  and not at my surroundings, when you judge me.
Don't you realize I'm the future of our race?
If I am lost, who takes my place?
If you hold my hand.
If you help me try.
If you teach me well and stop asking why.
If you can look past all else, all you should see,
IS A CHILD WHO NEEDS LOVE AND DIRECTION.
And that child is me.

Urban Schools Facts and Quotes

A hundred years from now
It will not matter
What my bank account was
The sort of house I lived in
Or the kind of clothes I wore
But the world may be different
Because I was important
In the life of a child

Compliments of Tennessee Education Association

Kirby High School

4080 Kirby Parkway

(901) 416-1960 - Main Office

(901) 416-1968 - Fax

Reginald R. Williams, Principal

Jason Jackson, Assistant Principal

Mannie Lowery, Assistant Principal

Daniel Jack, Assistant Principal

Annie K. Webb, Assistant Principal

The 4th Quarter

We have 44 days left before the state's test. Regardless of what the alleged predictions are for 186 city schools including 38 high schools, our focus are our students at Kirby High. I want our staff to remain positive, upbeat, and motivated. Our kids are resilient in many ways. Many of our students are doing well despite adversities they may face and many of them look forward to coming to school because of security, food, and shelter.

The 4th quarter, the 9th inning, the last leg (anchor) these final analogies mean we are in the <u>final stretch</u>. Yes, our attendance is important, coming to our classroom with a plan, a purpose, and yes, procedures to get there are important but the most important thing is <u>our attitude</u>. Remember, good instruction, interventions for our students who need that extra push and proactive discipline are the keys to success within our classrooms.

In closing, no matter how bad everyone says it is going to be (article enclosed); we can only control the results at Kirby High School.

As someone great once said, "be the change you want to see in the world" and continue to help our students reach heights they never thought they could.

5P's—Proper Planning Prevents Poor Performance

"Going from Good to Great"

A Message to Our Teachers

Ten Commandments
for Teen-Agers

1. Stop and think before you drink.

2. Don't let your parents down; they brought you up.

3. Be humble enough to obey. You will be giving orders yourself, some day.

4. At the first moment turn away from unclean thinking — *at the first moment.*

5. Don't show off driving. If you want to race go to Indianapolis.

6. Choose a date who would make a good mate.

7. Go to church faithfully. The Creator gives you the week; give Him back an hour.

8. Choose your companions carefully. You are what they are.

9. Avoid following the crowd. Be an engine — not a caboose.

10. Or even better — keep the original Ten Commandments.

P-429   Inter Collegiate Press

The Teacher

" I have come to a frightening conclusion. I am the decisive

element in the classroom. It is my personal approach that

creates the climate. It is my daily mood that makes the weather.

As a teacher , I possess tremendous power to make a student's

life miserable or joyous. I can be a tool of torture or an

instrument of inspiration. I can humiliate or humor, hurt or heal.

In all situations, it is my response that decides whether a crisis

will be escalated or de-escalated, and a student humanized or

de-humanized."

--Haim Ginott

National Center
for Family Literacy